the
Power
of
Circle

the Power of Circle

IMOGEN BAILEY

HAY HOUSE LLC
Carlsbad, California • New York City
London • Sydney • New Delhi

Published in Australia by:
Hay House Australia Publishing Pty Ltd, www.hayhouse.com.au
P.O. Box 7201, Alexandria NSW 2015

Design by Rhett Nacson
Typeset by Bookhouse, Sydney
Author Photo James Demitri

The author of this book does not dispense medical advice nor prescribe the use of any technique as a form of treatment for physical or medical problems without the advice of a physician, either irectly or indirectly. The intent of the author is only to offer information of a general nature to help you in your quest for physical fitness and good health. In the event you use any of the information in this book for yourself, the author and the publisher assume no responsibility for your actions.

ISBN: 9798318602283
Digital ISBN: 9798318605581

10 9 8 7 6 5 4 3 2 1
1st edition, March 202

The authorized representative in the EU for product safety and compliance is Penguin Random House Ireland, Morrison Chambers, 32 Nassau Street, Dublin D02 YH68, Ireland. https://eu-contact.penguin.ie

For my daughter, Odette, who reminds me every day how much we need each other.

We need to be held, supported and nurtured with love, attention and connection.

May she always know the magic of true human connection, Circle and community.

Contents

PART TWO **Every Circle Possible**

prologue

HELENA'S STORY

Helena was once terrifyingly alone, until she found Circle. For much of her 20s and early 30s, Helena looked like the woman who 'had it all'. She was envied for how together and successful she appeared to be. Her phone contacts were in the hundreds, and she was never short of a social invite, so why did Helena dread her reality every morning when the alarm went off?

Outwardly Helena was confident and friendly, with plenty of people in her life. Inside she was lonely, feeling no-one she knew was actually on the same page. It didn't help that she was dealing with a bullying boss at work, and stepchildren who seemed to know how to push all her buttons. With every day Helena fell deeper into crippling isolation, loneliness, and felt she was suffocating in the world, that she once believed to be enough.

In many ways it was enough. Helena had always wanted a family, a well-paid and stable job, and a nice home. But

Helena ached to find a true community, to experience a real sense of belonging, to feel heard, understood. In one of her darker moments, as often happens, Helena heard about a local Circle – a group of women who gathered every month to create their own sacred space, where difficult things could be talked about, laughter and tears could be shared freely, and where finally she could just 'be'.

The sad reality is, there are many 'Helenas' out there. There are women struggling with a toxic workplace, others navigating complex divorces, and others reforming after a life of social anxiety. And there are so many women who reach a point in their lives where it becomes glaringly obvious to both their hearts and minds that there is a much deeper self that needs and wants more and that self longs, excruciatingly, to connect with others who feel the same way.

With curiosity, clammy palms, and a desire for something 'more', Helena googled Circle, and what happened next was a game-changer in ways she never could have predicted.

The rest, as they say, is history – or is it?

INTRODUCTION: *My story, why Circles?*

Well, beautiful humans, this is me; my heart, soul and story out there into the big, wide world.

I'm Imogen Bailey; a Women's Circle educator, a birth and end-of-life doula, a meditation teacher and a Reiki practitioner. You might also know me from the other chapter of my life, as a model and actor. It might seem like two contradictory career paths, but in fact it makes perfect sense to me.

When I sat in my first Women's Circle, at the age of 32, I was in a huge state of transition, and also dealing with rejection. Relationship rejection, career rejection and societal rejection, or so I thought.

As we walk through this book together, you are going to learn a lot about Circle. I am going to guide you through ancient traditions, my modern-day musings, types of Circle, and both the benefits of attending Circle, and leading one yourself. Perhaps you picked up this book because you have a desire for connection, or you are desperate for a sense of belonging. Like me, you may be curious to build a business from Circle, with a desire to serve your community, or simply, there is a part of you that needs to discover a part of yourself that has gone on sabbatical. Whatever your purpose is, it's perfect.

Allow me to say, 'welcome home'.

I had done what it took to be a successful model (despite being a mere 5'3" in height). Despite wanting to be a lawyer or a journalist when I was younger, I had followed a self-paved path from celebrity television personality into an acting career. I had worked hard, I studied with great teachers and I climbed my way up the ladder.

In mid-2010, I found myself on a flight to Los Angeles, determined to 'break' into America. It didn't exactly go to plan – or maybe it did. Feeling defeated and exhausted, I soon stopped pursuing auditions. But I found myself on a healing journey.

I made some amazing connections with a number of cast members from my days with *Neighbours*, who were also in California at the time and found 'my LA village'. I discovered a local Buddhist community and creative women's groups, and this is where my search for self-acceptance began. I replaced my long standing rigid exercise and measuring routine with meditation and journaling. For the first time in a long time, I began to feel myself letting go and stepping into what I can only describe as my more natural and authentic self. **And then a friend asked: 'Have you ever tried a Women's Circle?'**

After my first Circle, I was hooked.

What I lacked in one part of my life, I found in the other. Loneliness became connection. Self-doubt became confidence. Hurt became healing.

Circle is a powerful and positive ritual that allows us to take women and men into a place where they reclaim their essence and their purpose, and they enhance their life condition/force.

Essentially we sit together in a circle formation and we create, play, share and recharge together just as the women in most cultures have done since the dawn of time.

While Circles throughout history took place very naturally, sadly it's a tool that for most of us has been long lost. So, the Circles of the modern world are an intentional experience that has to be rediscovered. These modern-day Circles may not necessarily include a group you have known all of your life, but they are just as powerful.

When the facilitator 'opens' Circle it has a number of meanings; to welcome new Circle participants into the room, to encourage an 'open mind and approach', to let everyone know they are in a safe and judgement free zone. From the opening moment, what is said and happens in Circle, stays in Circle. Once the Circle is open there is a feeling of instant equality and support, when you can all see each other's eyes and there is no hierarchy. In everyday life, we have managers we report to, partners who perhaps take the lead in a relationship, and sometimes, a divide in social status. However, in Circle, none of that matters. Circle is a space where everyday worries are put aside. Every single person in Circle is held, invited to be heard and embraced. In Circle, you will feel warmth in all its forms; in the heart, body and mind.

Circle is such a simple life tool yet becomes so significant to the participants' well-being, it is beyond measure. It is true what they say – 'when women come together magic happens'.

'We need joy as we need air. We need love as we need water. We need each other as we need the earth we share.'

– Maya Angelou

As a Circle of women it is an honour to share some of our life experiences and wisdom. And don't underestimate the skills you already have to offer women. There are as many ways to do a Women's Circle, as there are women. My hope is to offer you an introduction to Circle that includes some helpful structure and tools, so that if after reading this book you are called to explore Circle more deeply, you can add your own personal magic. Or perhaps you have known a little about Circles but have been afraid of the unknown factors and the new experience. I want to help you with any of those feelings too.

I now welcome you to the special world of Women's Circle.

'When women gather, magic happens.'

Sitting among a group of women, in my Ugg boots (Aussie slippers), with no make-up on and only a handful of tissues, I felt as though I had arrived home after an eight-year marathon of life uphill. For the first time, I felt comfortable sitting in my own skin. We shared our stories, without judgement or expectation. We paid homage to our mothers and our grandmothers (the known and the unknown). We didn't offer feedback, advice or sometimes even words. Our collective, subtle but all-consuming energy was magnetic. An integrative and exhilarating act of love. These Circles were changing my life. I was home.

Since then, the power of Circle has continued to amaze me and become a passion in my life.

I am now a mother who has overcome (*is overcoming*!) fertility issues, a wife who has learnt to trust and a woman who is attempting to shake baby weight after a high-risk pregnancy.

I am the creator of Honouring Heart, a community designed to help those with a similar passion to mine. I felt a calling, a purpose, to bring people back together in support and safety. I knew I wanted to explore the Power of Circle. We rarely sit uncomfortably in silence. Although we can hold space, I often wonder how much of that space is to validate our own worth, instead of boosting someone else's. Claiming to be an expert or guru is a dangerous myth. Some self-confessed spiritual leaders can get lost in the performance of ego and being a guide. The real skill in becoming any kind of facilitator or community leader is in the ability to hold a safe, equal, responsible and anchoring presence in a room.

Love does lead on many occasions, but with Circle we don't fix, advise, or hug without an invitation. Circle is not therapy, and I should add, I absolutely love therapy and respect my former therapists hugely. Circle is about being seen, heard and sitting in unedited and unfiltered honesty.

We listen. In stillness. Comfortably safe in the space we create together.

'What does it mean to hold space for someone else? It means that we are willing to walk alongside another person in whatever journey they're on without judging them, making them feel inadequate, trying to fix them, or trying to impact the outcome.'

– Heather Plett

Circle is a powerful tool that has incredibly powerful effects on people's mental and physical wellness. It brings people together and inspires creativity and soaring levels of self-esteem. Circle is for everyone, young, old, women and men. Similar to yoga and meditation, Circle should be available in every town and region around the world. This is one of my greatest ambitions – to never leave a spot in Circle unfilled.

Whether you realise this or not, you have come shoulder to shoulder with Circle. We have been practising the 'Circle Formula' for many moons. From tea parties and quilting groups to Bible study corners, eating disorder therapy groups, addiction support groups, wellness support for newbie mothers and rehabilitation meetings – they all have one ritual in common: to share story with like-minded people, to empathise and connect in order to heal.

In our busy world, where we have mental health issues screaming at us, we need to re-learn and reprogram Circle. Because we are so time poor, we have an app for instant everything; sex, movies, love, and a 4am ride (Uber) if we need it. Do we really want to continue being an instant existence?

Circle is an ancient and sacred ceremony, full of rituals and humanness. But it's also more relevant now than over. Over the next 50 chapters, I will deep dive into the healing power of Circle but also explain how you can take this feeling of connection out of a Circle and bring it into the rest of your lives.

I'll share my own journey with loneliness, self-doubt and the big transitions that have led me to this place. I'll also share incredible stories from women I've met in Circle and the challenges they have overcome. And, I'll challenge you to create a Circle in your world, whether it's with your loved ones or strangers – the community that is waiting for you.

❍ *I'm proud of my story*

When I launched Honouring Heart, my Circle facilitation business, I did it for one purpose, to unite women in story. Even today, when I am invited to media interviews, I have to think carefully about the parts of my past that I am willing to share. My story remains sacred, as yours should too. From my struggles overcoming an eating disorder, self-worth, success and failures, to fertility hurdles, I have always felt that my career was in storytelling.

I want my daughter, and your daughters, to grow up in a world united and not divided. And story is our vehicle to achieve this.

Today and every single day, I want you to know that your story is important and amazing. As I have become more settled in this statement, I hope you can too and that is to say: I love me.

All I ask is that you read on with kindness and compassion, an open mind and also playfulness. This isn't a practice that needs to be taken too seriously.

When I was going to auditions and casting calls, I never thought this would be my life's work. But I am all in on this passion journey of mine. I can't wait to gather you with me.

A note on the word Woman

I think it's important that I touch on something that has woven its way throughout my book and that is the number of times I have used the word 'woman'. This noun is how I identify. But in some Circles, I have welcomed men, and those who identify under a different pronoun. It is important that we adjust to inclusivity and acknowledge that everyone is welcome in Circle, regardless of their gender, religion, race, age or culture.

Circle is for everyone, and I mean, everyone.

Imogen x

part one

It's Not Just You

CIRCLE MAGIC – *what to expect; and shared miracles*

Over the years, either when scrolling through social media, talking to my clients, or sitting with my friends for a well overdue Chai tea catch-up, one phrase plays on repeat, 'I am not enough'". Society has asked us to be all the things; superheroes, warrior women, project managers to our own families, and formidable businesswomen, despite the toxic positivity that comes with wearing all of these hats (on very little sleep!).

In one breath, we are told to be stoic, and in the next, vulnerable. We grapple between grace and gregariousness, like the two are exclusive! Our friends tell us to 'speak our truth', while yogi gurus encourage us to 'let everything go'. It's no wonder we are all so confused. The perfect thing about Circle is that we don't align with labels, categories or job descriptions. Once and for all, we can just exhale, and be whoever we want, and need, to be.

❍ *Circle: let's go back to basics*

So, what is Circle? Circles are groups of women, and sometimes men, who commit to meeting as and when they choose, to create a truly safe and supportive space for each other. People seeking out Circle have a calling; a desire to recharge, relax, have fun, tap into their natural creativity (that we often forget we have) and share their stories together. They crave a place where they can dive into discussions and leave behind any social anxieties about being seen or heard that they may carry in the world outside the safety of Circle.

People also come together in Circle to acknowledge and celebrate a milestone moment in their lives, such as a birth or a wedding. Other people may gather in Circle to honour friendship, family, and even end of life. Regardless of the different types of Circle, the purpose is rooted in a desire to connect and belong in a safe sacred space; a place of equality, inclusivity, diversity and freedom. Circle is a judgement-free zone, where a person is bringing their truest self – spiritual or otherwise – 'label-less'.

So much can be gained from Circle as this is a place, your space, where you can be truly seen and heard. Where you can share things that weigh heavily on your heart and mind, that through other methods, simply cannot be untangled. Some people walk away from Circle bursting with clarity, and others feel calm and peaceful. Circle can evoke a sense of spiritual intrigue and curiosity, leaving a person asking, 'What's the purpose of life?' For others, they are happy to loosen their corporate persona and kick off their heels. I cannot stress this enough, there is no 'right' way to experience Circle. All I ask is that while you read this book, you leave your heart and mind open to whatever pops up! My hope is that through reading this book, you can fill up your spiritual cup with inspiration and knowledge, and lead your daily life with a sprinkling of Circle magic.

I am under no illusion that the life we lead today is starkly different from the ancient lineages I may refer to. After all, I am witness to the same headlines, struggles and demands as so many others out there. Circle has the power to do whatever you need it to. You may feel an instant and thunderbolt urge to transform your entire life (erm, congratulations by the way!), or you may want to find different ways to soften into hardship.

Ultimately, I hope to be that inspirational voice that says, 'You can live a different way, if your current life is no longer serving you.' But, as a realist, I know it's not always easy or possible to quit your job, live on a tropical island and live off the earth.

We all have responsibilities and people who are depending on us (the pressure!). However, the transition can be slow. The transition doesn't need to be radical or extreme. Circle doesn't ask for perfection, it asks for peaceful progress.

❍ *Storytelling behind the scenes*

I have never really closed the door on my career as an actor. However, as I turned the big '40', I did reach a point where I surrendered to the fact that perhaps my life wasn't destined for the dizzy heights of show business. Not because of my age, because as Australian actor Jacki Weaver will tell you, a big Hollywood break can come at any season in life. I just felt the need to travel more deeply in different directions from cold casting rooms and Los Angeles knockbacks. I confess it took me a moment to grasp that saying 'no' to the audition hamster wheel did not make me a failed actor.

It really doesn't matter what our accolades look like. It's about being in love with your craft, and for me that was understanding the power of storytelling.

An acting coach of mine many moons ago, Annie Swann, was a marvellous and wonderfully mysterious woman, who lived in the backstreets of Sydney's inner west. Her house was filled with incredible art and her wisdom was massively understated. She would say to me, 'Imogen, to truly act, is to find the story.'

This is the path for an aspiring actor, and not the bright lights and late nights associated with stardom. I would immerse myself in script analysis. I would become entrenched in the story as I untangled every plot twist and character profile. I thought this was only available in acting, but coming together in Circle opened me up to the ancient theories of storytelling too.

I like to think of storytelling as a vehicle to transport experiences and feelings. When we tell a story, we aren't asking for validation, agreeable feedback, or criticism, as the story becomes a boundary between the 'teller' and the 'listener'. Some stories are fictional, while others are 'real life' happenings, but either way, they appeal to our emotions. A story told well can last a lifetime, allowing history to tell it next. Through storytelling, we can deliver messages that other forms of communication cannot. A good story is imperfectly written, but can be perfectly told to remind us of what *really* matters.

From my childhood as a bookworm, storytelling became my passion and one of my few healing devices. Even as a birth doula (also known as a guide, support person and emotional comforter), the power of storytelling has a profound impact on the mother-to-be. Women are taught, mostly through the media, that childbirth is something to be feared. We are prepared for the horrific pain and the things that can go wrong. As birth workers, we tell and share the positive stories of hope, calm and connection.

Mythology and fairy-tales are not that different. If I said the name 'Cinderella', chances are you will know the innocent princess and the charming prince who woos her. Then there is 'the Fairy Godmother', the wise woman who saves her from the wicked stepsisters. These characters and others like them have been at the centrepiece of the stories from our childhood.

Whether you are drawn to fiction or non-fictional characters, they all play a symbolic role as to how we interpret humankind. Perhaps, if we shifted our mindset and looked at the world through a child's eyes or ancient myths, we could uncomplicate and understand life's magic.

I think about my life before Circle. I desperately needed a safe place, a warm place, a space for all the colours of my emotions and yearnings. A place where I discovered all the women I have within me: my wild woman, my wise woman, my leader, and the mother.

There isn't a woman I know who doesn't long for her version of this. A womanly version of the ancient stories and figures she carries inside her, that she can become. This version of womanhood is so much more than a character, but an untapped opportunity to truly release a side of herself that she has lost, forgotten, or truly never met.

And yet most modern-day women miss out on this ancient and magical tool. Where have all the Circles gone, I ask?

❍ *Circle: a modern-day kind of magic*

The purpose of a Circle is to assist every woman to receive support and empowerment to live her own unique life to the fullest. Many women suffer in silence from depression, loneliness and anxiety and science tells us that strong social connections have positive health protective effects. There are many kinds of Circles that are born from the needs of women. Support Circles; healing and wellness Circles;

community action Circles; spiritual/religious Circles. The effects of Women's Circles can be profound. For this reason women return again and again.

When women come together in a Circle they join together to embrace all in a sacred space and with intention. The Women's Circles of ancient times reflect the purpose of the modern Circle and connect those present in a singular purpose. Women share stories and work towards a deeper understanding of their own identity and that of the group. Sharing joy, working on projects or participating in sacred rituals all allow women purpose.

Think of the power when a Women's Circle comes together, where the participants share a dream for stillness, acceptance, equality and story. A dream that has the power to change each of their worlds. There are many forms of loneliness, with no one curable answer.

'If you find it in your heart to care for someone else, you will have succeeded.'

– Maya Angelou

'There were many things I would say to myself late at night or on my way home from work on the train. Some were negative thoughts, some were ideas and some were desires I secretly had for my life. I felt like I'd spent

most of my life editing myself or simply not speaking up about what I wanted to do with my journey. I attended my first Circle with Imogen in Sydney. For the first time I felt like it was completely OK to share all of my inner thoughts and not edit myself. I felt accepted, seen and connected to the other women in the Circle, who were having similar experiences to me. Circle changed my life and opened me up. Today I still attend Circles and I own my life!'

– *Chrissie*

'I felt like I had some mental health issues but no-one in my family wanted to hear me. I didn't feel like I could approach a therapist, because my family kept telling me I was OK and just needed to try and be positive about my future. I now know that this came from a place of love and not because they intended for me to suffer. Going to Women's Circles helped me find a safe place, where I could express myself. At the time, Imogen helped me find a good therapist. She told me Circle wasn't therapy but a "safe space holder". Looking back, I think Circle saved my life.'

– *Greta*

○

Circles and Grandmothers

I wrote in my mother's womb,
tapping out codes with my fingers and toes.
All the women clutching to our bloodline,
were reborn in the house my spirit calls home.
She was marked by me,
I was marked by her.
She carrying me,
I carried her.
Knowing touch and compassion,
free both fire and light.
We huddle together,
somewhere out there, way beyond time,
circling a sacred bonfire.
All learning to walk with gritted teeth,
on the hardened skin,
of each grandmother's feet.

Imogen x

○

'I can't sleep but that's because I am so happy and full of positive energy, amazing bunch of ladies tonight all sharing their beautiful wise energy.'

– Helena

chapter two

CIRCLE – *an ancient blessing*

Spiritual gatherings have been occurring since as early as 300,000 years ago. Over time, coming together in Circle and sharing practices have morphed, evolved, and taken on new purposes; however, the fundamentals have always been there.

Women in Circle have been healers, community leaders, medicine women, priestesses and sometimes even referred to as witches. We have even been taught to fear witches, to 'burn them at the stake', but was this because their power was so strong and deemed a threat? Sure, we have seen witches in horror movies depicted as the enemy, but is the word 'witch' just a massive misunderstanding?

Was it because their fierce nature had the ability to unify the feminine and dismantle patriarchy? Was it because these women, often so gentle too, had the ability to stand strong against opposition? I think so.

History tells us that when women come together to dance, cook, create art and share our powerful force, when we gather in Circle, anything can happen. When we exchange our experiences, we somehow dilute the harder times through empathy and non-judgemental ears.

When women take time to connect with their innermost thoughts and feelings they can better respond to their needs. This sacred space honours sexuality, prowess and femininity and is seen as a rite of passage to womanhood. The timeless tradition of gathering in a Moon Circle, is observed throughout many cultures and religions, and even today, women gather under the full moon, to receive the potent energy of the new and full moon.

Throughout many indigenous cultures, the union of sitting together in Circle gatherings, has been an old-time tradition to pay their respect to Mother Earth. From the Maasai in Kenya to the Native Americans and the Indigenous landowners of Australia, they all have one, distinct ritual in common – story time.

Yet, despite this, I've found that coming together in Circle can still be misunderstood. Because Circle can be more literal than you think!

People say, 'Oh, it's like sitting around a campfire, telling stories.' Yes, exactly like this. Sometimes there is a fire, sometimes there is a ring of flowers – the props don't always matter, but the principles do.

Do you remember as a child, when your grandmother would tell you stories about the war, or her first sweet love? The significance of passing down stories is part of our generational timeline.

Before the influx of smartphones and electronic everything, people only had the spoken word as a form of connection. In a world where we can access news at the swipe of a button, our own stories have become lost in the newsfeed. We mute, edit and script out our perfect captions to appear a certain way and this is perception versus reality.

The next time you are having a meal with your family, or brunch with your friends, tell a story. It doesn't have to be extreme or 'like' worthy. Instead recount a part of your past ancestry, that you hope one day, will be told again.

Circle is taking humankind back to basics.

At its core, Circle is a gateway, incorporating relaxation and self-care, intention setting and mindfulness. Circles are considered one of the first forms of social interaction, going back some 30,000 years.

Circles can be seen in many different forms, even if they don't go by the name of 'Circles'. We see women in Bible study groups gather for a purpose. Then there are Circles for recovery, such as Alcoholics Anonymous and Narcotics Anonymous. These are Circles where people exchange stories without pretence or expectation, and everyone holds recovery with absolute respect and anonymity. While our viewpoints may differ about what Circle can symbolise, the essence is to talk openly and freely,and be heard.

You might already sit in Circle regularly and not even realise it. Think about the times where you sit in curiosity and kindness with loved ones or strangers – this is Circle in action.

❍ *Where Circles began*

I'm going to be honest, if I hear the wind of a Full Moon Circle where I can dance naked in a forest under the vibrant moonlight, I'll be there! I know, it's not for everyone (and some Full Moon Circles take place in a comfortable yoga studio, fully clothed). I am going to fess up, I've never actually attended a nude Circle. But I want people to see the ease and freedom that Circle can create.

When it comes to Circle, there are so many types that – just like therapy – you shouldn't be put off if one doesn't feel right for you. There's a type for every taste, need and comfort level. As touched on earlier, Circle has appeared throughout the ages, in various forms.

That's why it is so important to acknowledge the various types of Circles, their history, origin and purpose. Over the course of my career as a Circle Facilitator, I have adapted my style on numerous occasions to meet my audience halfway. To offer them a sprinkle of 'woo-woo', that can be combined with perhaps, a conservative and more subtle experience.

Not every Circle you attend will make you fall in love with the concept. If it's not the perfect Circle for you, keep searching. I can safely say that we are not blissed-out bunnies. Instead, we practise openness and tolerance towards those who choose to share a sacred space.

The ancient ritual of Circle has essentially been a custom since people existed. Whether the gathering is to honour a menstrual cycle, a full moon, birth or death, women have been collecting in Circle for lifetimes.

And they are making a comeback. With wellness chats firmly on the radar in workplaces, gyms and societies again, it's now seen as somewhat trendy to form a Circle workshop of your very own. This is music to my ears. We are not trying to create anything new but revive the absolute power of Circle.

You don't need to be best friends with the person who is by your side. You may never see them in the outside world. These people don't need to be your best friends.

Sometimes, it's about sitting in Circle with people who you would never normally socialise with, to remind ourselves that we are all more alike than we are different.

'I've learned that people will forget what you said, people will forget what you did, but people will never forget how you made them feel.'

– Maya Angelou

'Embracing the sacred art of Women's Circles through Honouring Heart with Imogen Bailey, has not only become a catalyst for my personal healing but now, the foundation for my journey as a facilitator and entrepreneur. Today, as the proud founder of White Wolf Wellness Studio, I carry the essence of those transformative Circles into every facet of my life.

'Eleven years ago, my life took a pivotal turn as I found myself navigating the turbulent waters of a toxic marriage, with two precious children in tow. The decision to break free from that oppressive environment, marked the beginning of my journey towards healing and self-discovery. Seeking solace and understanding, I turned to a victims support service, yearning for a connection with women who had also weathered similar storms. It was during one of these vulnerable moments that I posed a question to my counsellor, "Is there a support group for women?" The response was disheartening – because there wasn't one. However, rather than succumbing to despair, a spark ignited within me that day. I was determined to create the community I so desperately sought.

'In the years that followed, my quest to establish a support network for women led me to the sacred art of Women's Circles. The inspiration struck when I stumbled upon a Facebook post by Imogen Bailey; a beacon of

wisdom in this transformative realm. I instantly recognised that this was the missing piece I had been searching for, so I embarked on a journey to study the sacred art of Women's Circles with Imogen. The course not only equipped me with the tools to hold space for women, but also instilled in me a profound understanding of the significance of gathering in Circle.

'The sacred work with Imogen has become a sanctuary for me, nurturing my growth and healing. My newfound confidence in holding space has also extended beyond the Circle of women to schools, kindergartens and various institutions where I collaborate with teachers, CEO's, charity leaders, and government employees. This journey has transformed not only my life but also empowered me to be a source of strength and understanding for those in need, weaving the sacred thread of healing through diverse communities.

'As I continue this journey, I am filled with excitement at the prospect of offering these sacred Circles, especially to women seeking empowerment and connection. White Wolf Wellness Studio is not just a business; it's a sanctuary and safe space where the transformative power of Women's Circles ripples out into the broader community. Circle touches hearts and fosters many healing connections. My vision is to grow a community of empowered women, creating a ripple effect of strength, support, and transformation that extends far beyond the confines of the studio walls.'

– Melissa

❍ A MOMENT FOR WISDOM

We are naturally a social species

Thanks to the self-help movement, there is so much advice on how we should behave as humans, it's unsurprising that now, we are just plain confused. One minute we are taught to be resilient, the next we are told to be vulnerable. In one breath we are encouraged to share openly, the next, to sit in silence. Women are taught to be boardroom 'go-getters', to then be ushered back into the nest.

When our friends fall apart from a break-up, we champion them to be free and single. Until loneliness and displacement sets in and then we are heralding how family life is a natural part of evolution.

If you don't know what way up is, then you are spot on.

In many ways, Circle is like the perfect spirit-level (no pun intended); a tool and way of life that promotes balance. When we live in a world of extreme everything; be it emotions, work/life balance, or social media fatigue, we all need a prop to smooth out the edges. Enter Circle, the place where we can totally slip into a natural state of being.

Sadly, there is no one right answer for everyone. Life is a mash-up of ancient traditions and modern-day adaptations. At the crux of it all, the one solid consistency is that, socially, we are not designed to live life solo. In fact, we are an 'ultrasocial species', according to Emiliana Simon-Thomas, PhD, Science Director of the Greater Good Science Center at the University of California. According to Simon-Thomas's research, she says, 'Our physiological systems have developed over the trajectory of evolutionary time in order to enable us to understand one another, to communicate in rich, nuanced, and granular ways, to coordinate our efforts towards broader goals that aren't possible to achieve at an individual level.'

This has never been clearer than since I became a mother, with a child who is entirely dependent on my life and care for their survival. In the world today it is also extremely clear that the loss of societal support has impacted most people to different degrees.

Since the dawn of time, we have relied on people to stay alive. Remember the famous movie *Cast Away* with Tom Hanks, whose character became deserted on a remote island after a plane crashed? He befriended a washed-up volleyball and was so desperately lonely, he later named the ball 'Wilson'. Soon, this object became his lifeline for support because he needed to interact with something, anything. He needed to feel less lonely, even though he knew how desperately isolated he was.

Being a social species will look like many things. Being a wife, mother, daughter, friend, birthing partner and best friend, all requires us to interact and react to a person who was once a stranger. We need to dig deep into our trust tanks, use our intuition wisely and learn how to work as one.

No-one wants to be in a position where we have to befriend a 'Wilson'.

chapter three

WHAT STORYTELLING HAS TO DO WITH IT

Effective storytelling isn't about blurting out every secret, problem, insight and piece of advice. It's a practice and essentially, an artform. You may choose to journal, a personal favourite of mine. Parting with words through a stream of conscious scribbling almost rids the burden they carried. If you have a gritty memory, causing you harm, I ask you to write it, read it and burn it (or safely tear it up). We've seen this played out in movie 'rom-com' rituals, as women tear up old love letters, or pictures of their ex. We've written poems to the people who've harmed us, with no intention of sending. We've made amends with our past traumas, without telling a soul! There is an almighty power in practically expelling pain, and putting to bed a story that no longer serves us. Perhaps this is the definition of 'letting go' that you've been searching for all this time.

Learning how to hold someone else's story or share your own is a BIG topic! The early days of how to do this can be super simple. Get (semi) comfortable with your words. Ground yourself by preparing a writer's nook. Think about the light and environment you plan to share your story in. Are you writing to share this story with a friend or your personal journal?

Most of my knowledge stems from my training when I became an actor, and it continues. I learnt, and continue to learn, how to impart a story that makes an impact. I have studied techniques on how to deliver a story's power, so that the audience can feel every inch of the plot. I did this by immersing myself in the characters I played and by drawing on my own experiences and storytelling abilities. But if I could say anything, it would be this: there is no score card to your story's worth. Whether your words are for you, a friend or a social media caption, think carefully about why you are writing them, and are the words coming from a place of an open wound or purpose?

If your story is your healing piece, this takes courage and I salute you. It takes bravery and faith to come from a vulnerable place.

If your story is a stepping stone in creating hope, I commend your willingness to write the bad bits down.

Your story is your superpower. Here are some helpful hints I have learnt along the way, – with some inspired by some of my creative friends – to help you on your first steps to storytelling.

Lessen the word count, not your truth: A well-constructed sentence can say so much, without sharing every personal detail.

Vulnerability versus regret: We can share details and still hold back. If you feel fear over freedom, it's not the right time to share.

Do not edit the parts that shaped you: Our honesty is not for everyone. But don't leave the milestones behind in fear of how they will be received. They made you, you.

The only 'like' that matters is yours: Painfully simple. Shockingly honest or honest to shock: We don't need to add content for click bait. We can be brave without bearing it all, in the hope that we will be noticed. Less in this instance, is most definitely more.

Don't harm but inform and protect your audience: Add trigger warnings and 'TMI' when needed to your post. Digital ears are hard to control but we can say the facts without illicit details.

Shake up the story, but not your boundaries: Cause a stir by all means; trigger a movement and a conversation. But don't let down your boundaries when they are most needed. They are there to protect you. Hear them.

Support the reader, and still protect your past: If your younger self was reading this, would they feel supported or siloed? You can reach out to those in need without full disclosure. Some secrets are still yours to keep.

Don't delete your story: EVER. And I mean, EVER!!!

❍ *I just needed to say it out loud*

Trust me, refraining from giving advice after hearing someone's story is not as easy as it sounds. And it's not an unnatural thing wanting to help someone struggling. Sometimes, we just need to say what is causing us anxiety and fear. Then comes the moment we have all become brilliant at ... filling the silence.

Silence can be a deafening obstacle in storytelling. Much like the end of a yoga class when the teacher says, 'annnndddddd, Savasana'. The final yoga pose to most yoga classes is called Savasana, otherwise known as corpse pose (bear with me here).

The purpose of this pose is to allow for all the good stuff to take place, after a sweaty and gruelling 60-minute flow. But it is in this moment, where all the chatter, the to-do lists and pressures slowly seep away. If we refrain from scratching our nose, or straightening our hair tie, we can fully immerse in the healing.

This is exactly the same when we need to fill a silence with advice giving. Our advice is not necessary when a person has the ability to unravel and untangle their answers over time. And hearing their story has the power to heal you too.

Storytelling is everything – it takes buckets of bravery to open up. It has only been in recent years that I have openly shared my former eating-disorder self. I know there is nothing to be ashamed of. I also know that I wasn't alone in keeping my weight at a scarily low level. I found, when I did choose to tell my story, so many other women came forward with theirs.

Perhaps you are bursting at the seams to shout at the top of your lungs and say, 'I am unhappy!' Internalising and suppressing the hard stuff can cause so much strain. I want you to know that you can be a widow who wants to find love, or a desperate woman on her ninth IVF cycle losing hope. If you are labelled the 'strong one' in your friendship group but feel anything but, share the down days. Open healing is not a burden because, trust me, others are feeling the same.

○

Circle is a place where you can say things out loud without editing yourself or worrying about what 'advice' you might be given.

❍ A MOMENT FOR WISDOM

The anti-gossip manifesto

'You'll never guess what I heard ...?' are the six words that can undo Circle. There have been behavioural studies on why we (men and women) gossip. It's been suggested that people can gossip in a positive way, out of concern for another party or to find a solution to a problem they're facing.

However, we've all experienced the other, darker side of gossip. This is where I ask you to be totally honest with yourself. Can you remember a time, where you were sitting with your colleagues, family or friends, and the conversation steered over to a particular person having received some nail-biting news about them?

We don't want to be seen as gossipers, but it can happen almost accidentally. It is not unusual to talk about people – the boyfriend who stayed out all night, the boss who pointed out a bad pitch, the friend who went radio silent on you. But how do you portray that pain? Do we single out the negative parts of a person to feel better about ourselves? Do we rob the reputation of a person because it unifies a conversation?

This can be a terrible, and harmful, habit. I try to live by these life-guiding lines from the book *The Four Agreements* by Don Miguel Ruiz:

- Be impeccable with your word.
- Don't take anything personally.

- Don't make assumptions.
- Always do your best.

In your Circle and collective of women, stand up for the person who isn't being supported. Enhance your life by gravitating towards people who want to see the best in people and speak the best of people.

If you find yourself gossiping, look at the motivation behind your words. Are you feeling insecure or jealous? Are you gossiping to fill an awkward silence? Are you doing it to feel part of a social group and, if yes, what could you do instead to find a sense of belonging?

In most cases, sharing more of yourself is more effective than spreading gossip about other people. Plus, it feels so much better to lift each other up instead of pulling each other down. Celebrate the bravery and big wins of those around you, the good, the bad and the perfectly imperfect.

chapter four

THE SELF-WORTH WORKOUT – *a beginner's guide to strengthening your self-esteem*

Happiness is a muscle. We must flex it like we would at the gym. Think of your worth, like you do your biceps. If we feed a muscle with negative affirmations, unworthiness and comparison making, that muscle is going to be ripped with regret. If we flex and feed the muscle with antidotes, self-love and reassurance, we are going to be pumped up with self-love.

The path to happiness and self-acceptance is a daily workout which requires dedication, commitment and kindness.

The women in Circle have become my workout warriors, and here is how.

❍ *Step One: Surrender to these feelings*

As a dedicated Circle Facilitator, when I bring a collective of people together, we sit as a group and welcome the spectrum of emotions. What we suppress, we liberate. We often can get tangled up in our emotions. We become afraid of the feelings that overwhelm, and transport us back to memories we would rather forget.

I am also going to say that getting super cosy with your feelings means learning the difference between surrendering and wallowing. Surrendering takes action, whereas wallowing can almost be easy. If it's always, 'life's fault', then what accountability do we have for improvement. We must remember that feelings will not harm us.

The trauma or fear sitting behind a feeling is immensely conflicting, but we hold the power with the emotion. For me, during turbulent times, I have chosen to stare a feeling in the face. It can almost be like 'buddying up with bad times', and 'getting to know' what role a feeling has in our lives. We can unpack the trauma, get to know its role, and close the loop by breaking the bond it has with us.

A simple way to do this, can be writing a letter to fear. Here's a little prompt:

'Dear Fear,

The role you are having in my life makes me feel like this …

Today, I choose to let you go by …

You no longer hold the power, and I am releasing you now because ...

Lovingly,
Me.'

So, I urge you to lean into the emotion and the 'dark night' without judgement or expectation.

❍ *Step Two: Explore trust with friends*

Vulnerability and trust can go hand in hand. To be our true and seen selves, takes courage. We are so used to wearing all the hats, masks and facades that protect us – our reputations, our ability to juggle families and full-time careers – that to be anything other than resilient can feel like a failure.

There is an invisible scale towards how to trust. At one end of the scale sits absolute protection, at the other is exposure. The trick here is to not commit to any spectrum, to not be *too* anything, but implement some helpful techniques on how to learn and earn trust.

❍ *Step Three: Be true to your word*

Follow through with positive actions: be selective with your choice of words, commitments and qualities. How we show up, says a lot about our own integrity. If we display respect for others, it is likely others will trust you in the process. With your work colleagues, family members and personal relationships, treat each interaction with kindness, empathy and always consider how your words and actions will land.

❍ *Step Four: Value the relationships you have*

Don't take them for granted. The people we choose to be surrounded by are not by perfect chance. None of us have a predetermined quota of best friends, partners and unbreakable bonds. If there is someone in your life who enriches your world, hold tight, show gratitude and respect that you chose one another. Complacency can sneak into our relationships, and we can assume that a person will just 'be there'. However, it's worth always reminding yourself, that you chose a partner, a best friend, and even a job because it or they, meant something to you. The next time you look at a loved one, remember it's just that, love.

❍ *Step Five: Work on your communication*

For the most part, communication is at the foundation of any trusting relationship, and bad communication is usually at the core of a breakdown. Sharing our feelings, both good and bad, offers no guarantees and doesn't come without risk. Observe how you communicate, in person, through text messages and even social media – every action is a message. The difference between good and problematic communication stems from intent. By understanding what we want from a conversation, phone call, or even a date night, can tip the scales between a beautiful time, or a bust-up.

❍ *Step Six: Always be honest*

I get it, this is a hard one. If it were easy, we wouldn't get so nervous or anxious when preparing to share a thought, feeling or even a dream. It is fair to say that some can use truth as a weapon, to hurt a person later down the line, or become a reason for your integrity to be questioned. This is where boundaries come in. Boundaries are not bargaining chips, but ways in which we protect our truth, and respect the feelings of others. Sometimes, preparing a script can be useful as a dress-rehearsal towards the big reveal. This could be asking your partner to share the household load, asking your employer for extra responsibilities or even telling a friend that you are considering IVF. We often play out a reaction to pre-empt our honesty, but what in fact happens, can shift the outcome in our favour. It's hard to argue with the truth, with little wiggle room for misunderstandings.

In Circle, we go within, assess our own insecurities, acknowledge they exist and straighten the crowns of our fellow queens.

❍

'We must be willing to let go of the life we planned so as to have the life that is waiting for us.'

– Joseph Campbell

Open your heart through movement and dance

Size of group: *3–20*
Time required: *15 mins*
Resources needed: *Writing materials and music to play. Be sure to find a song that really opens your heart when you play it.*

How the activity works: *Before the Circle dances, I ask that everyone places writing paper and pen next to them, and places one hand on their heart and one hand on their stomach. Where possible, it is a powerful prompt to suggest that the participants close their eyes if they feel comfortable, or drop into their bodies for the ultimate sense of safety and openness. You may need to explain the feeling of dropping into your body. This feeling can be achieved by breathing deeply and closing your eyes and allowing yourself to relax and feel deeply into your body. Explain that they might be able to feel the energy of life moving within their body. You may want to explain that it might take time and practice to completely allow these feelings in and that is OK. I then ask everyone to open a conversation with their hearts. We ask our hearts to trust, and be open in this moment. We then ask our hearts for some words that allow it to feel open or make it want to* *open. If we keep breathing and listening the words will intuitively come, like they are messages flowing straight from love. This is when we write the words down, before sharing with those in the Circle. This is when we stand, playing our song of choice. It's important to remember when doing an activity like this, that some people do not feel comfortable dancing. I might say, 'Feel free to start moving when you feel ready and if you don't feel comfortable dancing it is OK to sit or lie down and just feel the power of the music from your open heart.' I would also remind anyone dancing that there may be people sitting or even lying down.*

Prompt with this instruction:
I want you to begin to move when you feel intuitively called. Say the words you have written over and over and allow your body to embody and express these words through dance. I want you to naturally start to move in a way your body feels free. You can move your arms in motion, sway or twirl. I encourage you to be free, and to recite your words about love. Remember what your heart told you. Remember that you are completely alive in this moment.

Afterwards: *When the song comes to an end, have the women breathe and be still for a moment. You might then ask them to talk about how the activity felt.*

Sharing stories about our experiences can be both healing and enlightening and is one of the many beauties of Circle.

❍ A MOMENT FOR WISDOM

The spiritual roadmap activity

Inspired by a wonderful mentor, friend and teacher of mine, Helen Callanan, the founder of Preparing the Way, and who I studied with as an end-of-life doula is the Spiritual Journey timeline. I love creating this. I ask all of my Circle Facilitator trainees to pin the spiritual landmarks in their life. It's a simple but impactful method of seeing how emotionally we have unfolded as the women we are today.

The first part of any Women's Circle Facilitator training journey is really about you discovering how you arrived at where you are today. The hurdles that broke us, and the moments that elevated us to our next 'spiritual' level. I want you to deeply know yourself, so you will always have the confidence to know your truer self.

Take your time with this. There is no right or wrong way to do this activity. Be open with your past, with forgiveness and lots of compassion.

Grab yourself a sheet of paper and a pen, and mark in the following types of events with the symbols provided against your timeline:

A Star – A tool or skill set you have gained
A Heart – A turning point with a smile or sad face

A Tree – Something learnt from a family member or loved one
A circle – A breakdown or breakthrough moment; the ultimate paradigm shift

Understanding our unique paths, can determine how we came to be. This timeline will show you visually behavioural patterns, and the milestone moments in your life that have brought you joy, or even hardship. Use this timeline as a basis for what you want to see more of. Do you want more hearts than stars? Or is the balance right for you? By identifying the people we chose to connect with, or those we left, pushes us further into the places where we felt belonging. This task allows us to visually see how we confronted our past traumas, how we dealt with love and loss, how we have grown immensely over time and most importantly, how incredibly fabulous you are right now (even if you don't feel it today as you read this).

chapter five

WHAT TO DO WITH LONELY

Sadly, many of us at one point or another during our lives, have felt the pangs of living in a lonely world. This doesn't necessarily mean we have lived in solitude. Sometimes, roaming a busy city can feel lonely without friendship Circles, or a place to call 'home'. I have lived in some of the most vibrant cities in the world, including Los Angeles, New York, London, Melbourne and Sydney. During my career as a model, I was constantly surrounded by people – dressing me, styling me, chaperoning me. I had a full 'glam squad' at every photo shoot, not to mention the crowds of people at industry events and parties.

As I write this, I am a mother to a gorgeous little girl, living in one of the world's most famous cities, Sydney. I live in a built-up suburb, full of coffee shops, mamas' groups, and community hang-outs. I am never alone. But, that doesn't mean I'm not lonely.

Somehow, a busy metropolis can magnify physical, emotional and personal isolation. Somehow, becoming a parent can both fill your world with love and also illuminate the people who are no longer there for you.

Why? For the same reasons we as a generation are facing our biggest killer yet – the loneliness epidemic. No, you're not alone in feeling it. Loneliness is all around us, no matter what your life looks like.

For the first time, young people are being hit harder by loneliness than the elderly. As many as one in four Australians and Americans say they suffer from loneliness and this trend is mimicked around the world.

Loneliness affects our physical and mental health in ways you might not even expect – increasing a person's likelihood of depression or anxiety, impeding sleep and even reducing someone's life expectancy.

And where does it all stem from? I love the definition given by Letitia Anne Peplau, a professor of Social Psychology who studies loneliness. She defined loneliness as 'the unpleasant experience that occurs when a person's network of social relations is deficient in some important way'.

Do you have *deficient* social relations? Let's be honest, who doesn't! This is why we need Circle more than ever, and how I came to discover the power of Circle in the first place.

Surely, it's not just me?

Somehow, admitting you're lonely is still a taboo, even though (ironically) it is something we could bond over. We all know the feeling, we've all been there at times in our lives, the weeks when we feel like we haven't had a genuine conversation with another human being. The nights when you're scrolling the same social media content. Saturdays when you're wishing for the weekend to go by quickly because going back to work on a Monday is better than missing someone.

❍ *It's OK to say: I feel lonely right now.*
It also doesn't have to be that way forever.

It's also really not our fault. Society isn't set up for genuine connections anymore, in the absence of a 'village'. The message we're given, especially as women, is confusing. *Sex and the City* taught us we're meant to be strong and independent, but also have a girl gang who constantly meets for midday drinks. Facebook tells us to count our friends and never forget their birthday, but also doesn't prioritise real-world connection.

When we feel lonely, we are not always certain if we should tell anyone or do anything about it. It's easy to hide it, especially on social media. So, we take a photo of ourselves in our luxe loungewear, instead of admitting how depleted we are spending another night alone. We take a photo of the sunrise we see on our solo walk, and not the tears in our eyes.

People, more than ever, are afraid of loneliness – because we associate it with failure. Why don't you have more friends? Why don't you have more going on? Well, I'm here to tell you, that **it's not you, it's your circumstances. Society is lacking, you are not.** You can be an incredible woman with a thriving life, a successful career and a heap of hobbies and still have a missing piece. I am here for you and women across the world want to be there for you too.

❍ *There's not just one way to be lonely*

Loneliness is not solely exclusive for interpersonal relationships. Having experienced the tremendous struggles of infertility, I can vouch that creating a family with a noncompliant body has been one of my biggest personal battles. There is nothing more lonely than sitting in a doctor's office as they hand out the news that you've lost your baby – that the embryo, sadly, did not stick. I never had to undergo IVF, but after multiple miscarriages I can understand some of the struggles of those who do. I can relate to the loneliness of setting off to another baby shower or a girlfriend's big gender reveal – learning to smile and grieve simultaneously.

I am a firm believer that seeking out 'alone time' can be peace for the soul. In fact, being able to sit with uncomfortable emotions demonstrates growth. The end of a busy day, after putting the kids to bed or working a 12-hour day calls for quiet time. I personally love pouring a hot cup of tea, curling into my favourite corner on the couch and taking my first, conscious deep breath of the day. Some may choose to take a walk through the park and listen to their favourite podcast, enjoying their first schedule-free morning of the week. A friend of mine loves sitting on a bus (preferably in traffic jams) as it's her alone time between work meetings and cooking dinner for the family. Alone time is good. But where are the moments in between the two extremes? For me, it has always been Circle; a dedicated hour or two between bustle and bedtime.

Circle is a special spot; you are neither lonely nor alone but sitting among those who need 'their time'. A time to stop. A time to reflect. A time of zero pressure. A time to rub shoulders with a person who needs the exact nourishment as we do. These days, we live in an all-or-nothing culture; a black and white, instant way of seeing the world. Circle treats, welcomes, holds the loneliness that society strays away from without fuss, expectation or demands.

❍ *Avoiding stereotypes: we are all mothers*

We are living in an over-culture that says to be a woman, you must be able to produce children. I cannot stress this enough: incorrect. While I strived for motherhood, I came to terms and peace that perhaps this was not the path for me. As young women, and men, we are taught about the roadmap to adulthood: get educated, be successful, settle down and procreate.

There is a societal narrative, that all women make babies. When I disclosed my miscarriages to my family, I felt like I was failing as a wife and a woman. But it wasn't my family who was judging me, it was me judging me. I thought, 'Who am I going to be, if I can't have a family?' My modern brain knew that wasn't real, but my inner chatter was beating me down at every point.

This is when story versus storytelling are very different.

We can all create 'a story' in our head – a series of catastrophic events that are not based on truth. In the absence of facts, we fill the gaps with negative plot twists. When I experienced three miscarriages, my story wasn't to feel self-compassion, but that I was, in some way, less of a woman.

Robb and I prepared ourselves for the space that may lie ahead of us in the absence of children. We decided that we would travel the world, and love our nieces and nephews wholly. So, loneliness can look different individually and as a family.

Here are some other ways loneliness can impact us:

Life transition loneliness: You have moved to a new city, country, workplace or school. Surroundings are unfamiliar and nothing feels the same. You are sitting in the work lunchroom on a table alone, or pinning the closest grocery stores on Google Maps. You have moved inland from the ocean and cannot hear the waves crash like you used to. The faces on your commute are different and less friendly-looking. Geographical and circumstantial loneliness is real but resolvable.

Parental loneliness: Conversely, becoming a mother for the first time and understanding how to keep a tiny human alive and healthy, is a lonely place. The pressures for perfection (despite nothing of the sort existing), are extra pressures no newbie mum needs to experience.

Heartbreak loneliness: The same could be said for relationship breakdowns. We have all been there. We find a person who becomes 'our person'. You have fallen in love, exposed your partner as being 'the one' to family, friends and social media and then one day, you find out the worst.

'I've made it' loneliness: A successful job offer, a promotion and achieving professional goals can be equally as isolating. Perhaps you have been nudged up the ladder, where your former workmates are now your subordinates. Your colleagues are now avoiding you at the water cooler, or cutting conversations prematurely in a bid to get away from deadline chat, envious of your massive bonus pay cheques. Your professional elation is now an isolated walk into the office, and despite revelling in achievement, you wish it would all just go back to 'normal'.

'He's the one' loneliness: Oddly, being in love can be a lonely place. Navigating relationships is probably an entirely different book but it has to be said that in the early stages of a new romance, understanding how the other feels, is like steering a ship without a map. Do they like or love me? What is wrong with me? Why are they still acting single but seem so invested in making me happy?

'I don't fit in' loneliness: We crave bonding. We are hardwired to relate to those around us, despite always wanting to rebrand ourselves to stand out. You could be living in a bursting-at-the-seams household, but no-one listens to you at the end of a long day. In fact, the louder the TV or radio, the more isolated you feel. You could have been diagnosed with a rare condition that riddles you with shame. You could be Christian in a house of agnostics. You could be gay, in a staunch homophobic community. The degrees of difference vary, but none are any less lonely than the next.

We can feel like we're the only person who feels this way. If only we could also find a way to connect, to reunite and to share, we would know we're all going through the same things daily. We're all far more alike than we are different.

A MOMENT FOR WISDOM

Being busy will fix it

Myth One: Distraction is the cure

When we feel lonely, how many of us add more to our schedule to solve the problem. Sometimes it helps but often it just papers over the cracks. Now, you're exhausted *and* lonely! We are conditioned to think that success is being on the move – to always have somewhere to be and people to see. It is an exhausting performance that none of us are truly qualified to do.

The next time you feel lonely, I challenge you to do *less* and not more. To remove one thing from your schedule, not add to it. Yes, it's going to be uncomfortable. You're not going to want to but guide yourself to do it. This is the first step in getting to know yourself. Which brings us to Myth two ...

Myth Two: Excitement is the goal

How much of your loneliness is driven by comparison? We see other people's 'exciting' lives on social media and start to think ours is not enough. We don't celebrate contentment – a state of happiness and contentment – often because you have everything you need. Instead of wishing you had more, including more people in your life, how can you lean into contentment instead? This is where a gratitude practice can be powerful. Every morning when you wake up, think of three things you are grateful for today.

The goal is to stop chasing the thrill of excitement and realise that contentment is amazing and very underrated. My most contented moments are sitting feeding my baby alone, just me and her. I cherish every moment when I can walk in nature, or share a meal with my hubby when a busy day ends. Sometimes, contentment for me is sitting in my daughter's playroom or the bathroom, cramming a quick two-minute meditation in before my daughter wakes up. It certainly doesn't look exciting to an outsider but in that moment I have everything I could need. Ask yourself this: How am I going to just be in my life with my thoughts and attempt to find peace?

Myth Three: Being alone equals being lonely

Being alone can actually be a place of complete surrender and peace. Be it a choice or a place that you have arrived at. I have met so many women over the years as an Honouring Heart Circle Facilitator, who are screaming for alone time. These women are busy at home, leaders at work, and the solo parent designated to school drop-offs and pick-ups from parties. Sometimes, the feeling of overwhelm (and loneliness) can be an inside job, with daily anxiety taking residence in a busy mind, screaming for freedom. If you are feeling lonely, commit to spending *purposeful* time alone, in a way that you really enjoy. Remind yourself how wonderful it is to be alone, when it's on your terms and because of your choice.

Schedule a solo walk to listen to a podcast, go to the gym and don't join a workout class, or take yourself out for lunch with a book to read. It can take practice to go somewhere alone, especially if you're a parent who is used to having at least one little person pulling at your arm.

Important check-in question: Do you feel alone or lonely?

'As a mum to three young children; a two-year-old and then premature twins, I felt very lonely and disconnected from society. During the lockdown period, this intensified and I decided to do Imogen's Circle Facilitator Course. After completing the course, I started running online Women's Circles. I loved it! I started running Circles from home once a month, and have been doing them for a few years now. The numbers still fluctuate, but they are always a beautiful experience. I recently started running a monthly Saturday afternoon Women's Circle at a local community centre, and I hope it will grow too. Being a Circle Facilitator is an absolute gift. The women I have met are incredible. Everyone deserves some time to feel relaxed, supported, nurtured, connected and uplifted, and that is what I aim to provide at each Circle.'

– *Nicole*

A MOMENT FOR WISDOM

Easy, not so easy, does it

After witnessing the atrocities in Somalia and Indonesia while on location filming *Go Back To Where You Came From,* I was craving home. I was craving my mother's love and care. Being an independent woman can be exhausting.

Being part of this incredible documentary series, I joined a group of Australians to discover, discuss and dismantle the asylum-seeker debate. We went on a life-altering journey to discover and understand the crippling and drastic measures a refugee will take to find safety in Australia.

Our resilience becomes our identity, until it becomes our burden. Just because we can be survivors, doesn't mean we always want to be. So, I decided I needed to replenish and go back home to Australia. This is when I decided that I would explore my calling, to help women find theirs.

After returning home from overseas, I remember how hard it was to shake off the mental images a city like Mogadishu can imprint. More importantly, I didn't want to. I didn't want to be a one-time crusader or someone who would learn, close the lesson, and move on. If I didn't use the opportunity to make my own changes it would have been a massive injustice to addressing lawlessness and suffering. I would have confirmed the beliefs of my worst critics, that I was poorly informed and uneducated.

The women at the foodbank in Somalia didn't see a blonde girl with a celebrity backstory, they saw me, a woman. These women were broken, defeated and desperate. Even fathers begged me to take their starving children. When these people could have given up on each other, they came together stronger. Women would hold their limp and starving children, lining up for rations, and place a hand on the next woman's shoulder to show love, reassurance and hope. They smiled at me, like *really* smiled. The Circle of support they created for each other couldn't feed them, but it held them while they waited for supplies.

On one stretch of road, wreckages of plane crashes lined the streets. I remember turning to my producer and saying, 'If I could fix this plane, fill it with people and fly it to safety, I would.' I was never going to become a pilot, but I knew I had to help women.

Back at my mum's house in Sydney, I started researching how to become a doula. The word 'doula' comes from ancient Greek, meaning 'woman's servant'. It's not a woman who happens to be a servant but a woman committing to serve, though we do make cups of tea when required. My newfound purpose led me to Renee Adair, Founder and Director of the Womb to Tomb foundation. I instantly knew that I wanted to follow in her footsteps.

I knew from my time on *Go Back to Where You Came From*, women as refugees and asylum seekers are left to face the burden of giving birth alone. Back then and even now, Australia doesn't have the support systems to help women who have been detained by the government. Once they give birth, they will be placed back into detention.

Renee, also founder of the not-for-profit, Doula Heart Network in Sydney, was my perfect teacher. She was nurturing, compassionate and a fierce advocate. The way she spoke about birth and caring for families and babies, was so deeply entrenched in heart language, that I knew I had to learn from her. Her passion was infectious, and I felt completely held in her presence. In one of our conversations, she told me that she had been born in the same hospital as my mum. It was a sign. Some say, looking for a sign is a sign, and this was my compass to lead a life of heartfelt service.

I remember while training with Renee, we sat in a Circle and lit a candle for our mothers and our grandmothers, those known and unknown. It was a deeply moving experience and one of the steps that led to me later teaching Women's Circle.

For some, being a birth doula, a non-medical support person who nurtures and assists women and families through pregnancy, labour and birth, or after you have your baby (postpartum), makes complete sense. It is seen as a comforting and celebratory role to support a woman as she becomes a mother. After meeting Helen Callanan from Preparing the Way, an end-of-life doula, I learnt that birth and death mirror one another. Both are significant landmarks in a person's life, and as a doula, we pay respect to how we welcome life, and farewell it. In a way both of these mentors showed me another layer to Circle and they both used Circle rituals in their training that inspired me. The Circle of life and the Circles of support go hand in hand.

chapter six

WOMEN NEED TO TEND AND BEFRIEND

❍ *What happens when we get lost in our head?*

Over the years, I have spoken to thousands of women with one common and unhelpful story: I am not enough.

It can be a vicious cycle. Our self-worth is low so we don't feel confident in social situations, especially with women. Sadly, the lonelier we feel, the greater our self-worth struggles. And so on, and so on.

But it doesn't have to be this way. In fact, by strengthening our ability to connect with the right people, our sense of worthiness gets the boost it is longing for. And when I say the 'right people', I mean those who give you a sense of safety, friendship, and those who you trust. These people can be family members, or even colleagues, but when we surround ourselves with those like us, empathy and connection will always prevail. In fact, research shows that a sense of belonging is crucial to our life satisfaction, happiness, mental and physical health, and even longevity.

Like most things, the journey starts with (cliché alert!) learning to love ourselves. There's a reason it's said so often, because it's true. So, how can we get there?

The stories we tell ourselves

Often, we tell ourselves any story, even the unhelpful ones, just so we can fill in the missing blanks to answers out of our control. It feels safer to make up a story that reflects our self-worth, rather than waiting for accurate details, despite the negative impact this can have. When we are feeling threatened, or unsure of ourselves, we will conjure up a story that doesn't always match reality. Before we know it, we have formed a 'story pattern'; first comes the fear, then we imagine the worst, and before we know it, we have imagined a devastating outcome. This pattern is founded on fear, rather than reality. It's a form of self-protection, where we can outrun a problem that, in fact, hasn't even happened.

A really helpful acronym to keep in your back pocket is, 'FEAR': false evidence appearing real. If you feel yourself beginning to catastrophise with imagined terrible outcomes keep repeating the acronym for FEAR until you feel a separation from the bad thought train occur.

Have you ever sat with your friends and worried about how your new love interest is ignoring your messages, even though he's always online? Why aren't they responding to us? We assume they're not interested in us, which could be true, but do you have any real evidence? Or is it 'FEAR': false evidence appearing real?

We can do the same with our friends or colleagues. One strangely worded email and we think we're about to be rejected or fired!

Our self-esteem is eaten away, every day, by the stories we tell ourselves. It is our responsibility, every minute of every day, to challenge ourselves when we think the worst of ourselves. When that thought pops into your head, pause and think: What's more likely to be true?

How would you talk to someone you love, such as your best friend? How can you start to see yourself with the same compassion?

❍ *Be your first love*

My Circle sisters, hands down, are in their own perfect love affair – and it's brilliant to see. They love themselves, deeply and also gently, because they have committed to doing the work! They still have hang-ups and bad days, but generally they know they are incredible and powerful women who are not perfect but are worthy of everything good that comes their way.

Putting yourself first, can sometimes come across as selfish behaviour. We become our number one priority as we steer towards a healthier mind. However, there is a massive difference between selfish and selfless. Being selfless to a happier you is the greatest gift you can give yourself, and the people around you. Personal development is not a one-way street but a domino effect that will impact your family, friends, and workmates.

I often say, my mental health is the greatest asset I have, and it's non-negotiable when forming new relationships. By setting fierce boundaries you are in fact, creating boundless honesty. Carving out an hour, even five minutes, in your day to check in with your well-being can be the difference between a breakdown moment or a much-needed breather in a household of chaos. When you have become the go-to friend for last-minute childcare, instead of saying a big, fat yes in the mindset of a meltdown, I want you to say, 'I cannot help you today.' When your ex-partner assumes the rights of the child, fairly explain that you are, in fact, equals. When your boss wants a task completed 'ASAP' when the clock hits 5 p.m., grab your bag and leave. These are everyday examples, but fundamentally, you are being respectfully firm.

I can safely predict that this may be met with feelings of guilt as you reshuffle the order of priorities in your life. But I urge you to let that go. This doesn't mean skipping the important parts of your day, such as family mealtimes or taking your children to school. This could be booking a yoga class you've had your eye on for a year or meeting a friend for lunch who you've cancelled multi-times due to busyness. For some, this may go a little deeper.

Has your yearning to find more meaningful connections become greater every day? Have you known that your current support system is failing, and you are desperate for help? Permitting time to improve your mental health is a pure act of love. Don't mute the parts of yourself that truly believe something needs to change in your life. Falling in love is an incredible feeling, and there is no greater relationship to daydream over, than the one with yourself.

❍ *Watch out for red flags*

I always want to encourage everyone to be responsible for their own emotions. I don't love blaming other people for how they make us feel, however there are some relationships that are downright toxic. When our self-esteem is low, we can find ourselves in them, for all the wrong reasons. I know it is hard, but sometimes you do have to walk away.

I had two-long term relationships before meeting my husband. In my late teens, I was with my first boyfriend for eight years. Unfortunately, I think we were both in different relationships. After learning of his many betrayals, I was crushed. He was my world. I had become part of his family.

His future dreams and our time together had spanned my teen years to early adulthood. He was all I ever knew about how to be a girlfriend.

After the relationship broke down, I promised myself that my next boyfriend would be different. We have all been there – 'The next time it's on my terms, my timeline and no-one will ever hurt me again.'

Wrong.

Succeeding as a model was my revenge tactic against boyfriend number one. I thought to myself, 'I will show him. I will show him what he lost.'

After some short-term relationships, I found myself head over heels in love with a handsome and charming actor. This time, I vowed to ensure my needs were met.

But again, I found myself in an unfaithful relationship. Betrayal was starting to be the only thing I knew about love.

At the time, I thought my career was 'failing'. Now, I see it with an entirely different lens. To the contrary, my schedule was always fully booked. The producers didn't stop calling, I stopped answering the phone to them. At the time, my self-esteem was so low that it felt easier to hide than to really show myself and be successful.

My career was officially stalling and I was back in the vicious cycle of a toxic relationship. Eventually, I spent all my savings on 'us', skipped auditions and stopped taking care of myself. I am the first person to acknowledge that what we want, we ultimately invite. But sometimes what we want, and what we have left in us, is too big a margin to narrow. When we are at capacity mentally, emotionally and physically, and still strive for more, is it any wonder we crash? I suspect not. I would ask my friends and myself, 'Why am I still putting up with it?' I knew, deep down, I was worth more. But, if you spend a long time in a 'not quite good enough' state of mind, it can quickly become part of you.

In both situations, I did what I thought would please the other person. I changed myself, from the outside.

Change #1: I always had good teeth but apparently my teeth were *too* small. I remember my first boyfriend saying, 'You don't exactly have "Macleans" teeth do you?' I got myself new and bigger teeth simply to please him. I would later break my new teeth while filming *Celebrity Survivor* in 2006.

Change #2: With a Nordic and Irish heritage (with a bit of Spanish and French flung in there), I am naturally very blonde. For one modelling campaign, I dyed my hair to become a brunette. My boyfriend saw pictures of the campaign that was from before we were together and he loved the look so much that one day he said, 'I wanna meet *that* girl.' So, I again dyed my hair to become a brunette, despite not liking it much myself.

On both occasions, I changed how I looked because I thought it would make me feel more than I was. More loved, more respected and perhaps safer with the other person. But it never does. They were betraying me, and I was betraying me too.

If you find yourself negotiating parts of yourself that you love and adore, this might not be the right romance for you. If you find yourself changing the outside, to mend what's inside, any adoration will be skin deep and frail.

This isn't where I urge you to take action against a relationship that sits on rocky ground, but I will ask you to tap into your truth. Is this love or loneliness with a guaranteed partner?

Choose you, beautiful. Like, *really* choose you. Deep down, there will be a feeling (instinct) you should listen to. Are the unhappy days outweighing the good? Do you wake exhausted thinking about yet another difficult day ahead? When was the last time you felt at peace in your skin? What's on the flip side of a big decision is a big and incredible life.

❍ *Do you sense a fight, flight or freeze response?*

We all naturally respond to stress in different ways, however a common reaction to feeling overwhelmed is to fight, flee or freeze. The 'fight or flight' concept, coined by physiologist Walter Cannon in the 1930s, exposed how men react in adversity. But with studies predominantly researching the male reactions to upset, a missing piece of the puzzle was uncovered – how do women react under threat?

Now, a new theory has emerged – to 'tend and befriend'. According to psychological and scientific studies, tend and befriend is the instinctive reaction where we are compelled to nurture (to tend) and find a safe and loving sanctuary (befriend).

When faced with tragedy or suffering, the average woman will have a greater tendency to protect and shield the young and find comfort and strength in their social networks. Basically, our natural urge is to gather – so why are we pushing against it?

With society sending us messages that resilience, independence, and conquering life alone is what makes a woman a fierce woman, we have suppressed this stress response in fear of judgement. But beneath the surface of a steely exterior, we are all craving unconditional love.

Nurturing someone, or something else, is also incredibly healing.

After I experienced a series of miscarriages, my husband and I welcomed a rescue dog into our home (Bruno, a shy and anxious Harrier). We knew the uphill struggles we were facing with our desire to extend our family, but in the interim, we needed to outsource our love, and provide a protective home for an animal in need.

Whether you have children or not, this primal desire is in all women. When our friends and loved ones are facing hardship, we don't impulsively pack our bags, weapon up, jump in the car and flee. We rally. We call on our friends via a group chat, plan a comforting night in and tap into our village of supporters.

We nurture, shield and love. Now, this isn't to say men do not do these things, but the response of a woman is often to soften and not combat the difficult.

We don't need to write a fix-it manual on every bad day, but simply be. Easier than it sounds, I know. But so much can be gained from sitting in stillness and silence, if we allow the process to breathe.

'I decided to train as a Circle Facilitator, as there wasn't anything available in my area. I wanted to create a community that I could be a part of, to bring women together to just "be"! I joined forces with a friend of mine who is a Reiki healer and trained in crystal healing and is a psychic medium, so it made the perfect fit. Now we co-facilitate and I do sound healing, meditation and human design, so we complement each other, to bring a beautiful experience to our Circle of women. Circle has brought me so much joy connecting with like-minded women; holding space for them, safely. When the weather is warm, we do our Circles outside at a local oval and in the cooler months, we hire an indoor space.'

– Bronte

❍ A MOMENT FOR WISDOM

Five signs you're craving female energy

- **Take me as I am:** Humans love to be loved. Many of us still feel incomplete, even when our social schedule is bursting at the seams. There is nothing more satisfying sometimes, than staring at our calendars packed with brunches, lunches and cocktail hours with the girls. But are you living your truth? Social circles and in-person connections nowadays are comparable to social media networks. We are having to project a certain image in order to keep our seat at the table. What if we could turn up to our next diary date, unfiltered, unedited and unapologetic about it?

Satisfy the craving task #1: When someone asks how you are doing? In one word, tell them exactly how you are feeling. PS, 'busy' isn't a feeling.

- **Longing for story:** My favourite teacher and author of *Women Who Run with the Wolves*, Dr Clarissa Pinkola Estes, says, 'Nothing less is needed on our planet at this time.' And she is so right. Our planet is struggling, and we have become a culture that no longer relies on personal interactions in order to thrive. To share a story and *really* listen, is one of our greatest and most forgotten gifts.

Satisfy the craving task #2: Is there a book you have been meaning to buy, or struggling to find the time to read? Carve out just ten minutes each day, find a quiet corner, and open a page.

- **Smiling on the outside:** Perhaps, something inside you, has become fascinated by the meaning of inner intuition. Tapping into your inner power or divine femininity is essentially 'googling' within. Have you ever uttered the words, 'Damn, I wish I had listened to my gut'? When we have become so digitally reliant on how we should feel, work, cope or follow, living by a list of 'shoulds' rather than 'needs' is preventing us from living.

Satisfy the craving task #3: The next time you are tempted to go against your instinct, I challenge you to stop, listen and reverse what your head is saying. Instead, listen to your heart.

- **Tend and befriend:** Research heavily suggests that the opposite response of 'fight-or-flight' is to 'tend and befriend'. When we are under threat, our response can be to rush towards confrontation or to flee it. This is where we can change our thinking to avoid tackling a problem alone. Calling on your sisterhood can help resolve traumas and not escalate them.

Satisfy the craving task #4: If you find yourself in a period of personal or professional conflict, consider if this problematic load can be shared. Who do you trust with your darkest days and who can support you through hardship? Trusting your people can be the difference between resolve over ruin.

- **Dig a little deeper:** Knowing your past, is knowing your present. More than ever, we need to pay homage to our ancestors, as opposed to steamrolling ahead in a fast-moving world. Knowing where you came from; your traits, traumas and triumphs could be formed by part of your heritage. Subconsciously, you may be drawn to a certain symbol, purpose, gift or calling. Did your grandmother and mother feel and heal the same?

Satisfy the craving task #5: Ask your mother, grandmother, sister or aunty if they felt a calling to Circle or an experience that looks or sounds like modern Circle. Perhaps a knitting group or book club if not a traditional Circle.

- **It's a family thing:** Perhaps the women in your heritage have felt similar feelings, or a longing for belonging. The next time you speak with your mother, grandmother, sister or aunty, seek out their experiences of disconnection, and most importantly, how they found their inner Circle.

Satisfy the craving task #6: Talk to one woman in your family or a close friend's Circle and ask them to tell you a story about making or meeting an important friend who changed or deeply enhanced their life. Pay attention to their facial expressions, especially their eyes. You will see the magic of true connection being told and feel why it is so important to us.

chapter seven

WOMEN NEED WOMEN

So much of our past can shape us, but our worst memories and triggers do not necessarily have to define us. We are all searching for a place where we belong; a friendship circle, a mums' and bubs' group.

I spent much of my early career surrounded by actresses and models, so there was no shortage of female company. But female company and female energy that can heal us, can be two, very different, experiences.

It was not unusual to step into an audition casting with a room full of beautiful and confident women. I never believed I shouldn't be in that space, but I certainly doubted if I was good enough for it. I don't think I was the only one feeling this way, because sadly, most of us tend to be victims of 'Imposter Syndrome'. This is the inner chatter that we are incompetent or that 'someone will figure out' that we are struggling with a lack of self-belief! But it doesn't have to be that way.

Finding and confiding in women can offer safety and trust.

❍ *What it means to truly support one another*

I have unravelled my past, shared my meltdowns and dissected the hardships with you. Now I want to mobilise us as a collective of powerhouse superheroes. OK, that may be a little too much but I do want us to relearn the lessons and tools for a less lonely life. I just know that together we can do hard things, and the time is now.

One particular phrase I love is, 'It takes a village to raise a child.' Originating from an ancient African proverb, this wise old saying promotes the concept that to raise a child, or survive as a family, requires help from outside of the household.

I've heard this famous phrase used in playgrounds, Facebook posts, mama blogs and even in top-notch advertising. Yet, I do worry that ideas of a village have become a thing of the past for a lot of people.

Over time, we have mastered mayhem quietly. We don't leave our backdoors open anymore or act as automatic guardians to the children next door. I'm pretty sure the first half of this phrase, 'It takes a village', is as important for single city dwellers, as it is for growing families. Not only are we living life solo, we are crippling under the pressure to nail parenthood and partnership single-handedly.

Not every bumper sticker statement resonates. You may feel that the term 'village' doesn't resonate with you. So, let's modernise this concept and harness help in different ways. Perhaps you are part of a social network that forms a hobby, or the creator of a support club, but either way, this is in your village.

Even though my life has strayed away from the public eye, it's no less chaotic. If anything, raising a child in a quiet suburb two hours from Sydney's busy metropolis (we moved to the South Coast from Sydney when my daughter was seven months old), requires extra support more than ever. Running a business, being a mum and a loving wife, means that sometimes I do less for me and need my resilience more. And I'm guessing (no matter what your version of the chaos is) you know exactly what I'm talking about.

Let's get our villages back up and running, one simple hello at a time. This is where I want to 'circle' back to Circle. Nowadays, our villages are a little harder to find, in the urban jungles of a busy metropolis. But even in the busiest of places, Circle can exist. It's just looking that little bit harder to find your soul family. And when you do, which I know you will, you might just find yourself sitting in a Circle and having the same epiphany I did – a return to Circle is the beginning of reclaiming the village-like support we all so desperately need.

My simple steps in learning how to discover your people:

It doesn't happen overnight: Friendships and meaningful connections take time. Your best friend or partner were once strangers, until your magnificent self made an impression on them.

Be prepared to take yourself out of your comfort zone: As we grow older, we get super comfy, super fast. We tend to stop 'putting ourselves out there'. Stepping outside our comfort zone is where we learn, remaster and trust new people.

Start with hello: When I go for a walk, I am prepared to say hello to a complete stranger. Starting with small talk is OK because the bigger chats will come.

Make eye contact: This can sound a bit creepy (and obvious), but trust me, purposeful and intentional eye contact allows a person to be truly seen.

Maybe a little something more: Great, you have nailed your first 'hello'. At this point, the person opposite may walk straight past, respond or even better, comment on the weather. It doesn't matter. At this point, you are creating a connection with a person who has been sitting alone at work for the past five days, or going through a tricky time. Become the cheerleader to your and even someone else's confidence.

These simple actions for many, can feel a little obvious. But interacting with strangers is like polishing our bravery on a daily basis. I want to say, always feel safe with anyone you spark up a conversation with. Remember it's just a chat. Not only did the pandemic force us into isolation, but the digital boom of virtual living has dampened our interactive skills and that isn't looking like it will slow down in the near future.

If you have built an empire, a successful career, your family home, or a romantic relationship, now's the time to build your village outside of certain relationships. We are in desperate need of rewiring, relearning and rebooting our ability to learn true closeness.

It all sounds super basic. And in many ways it is. I am not wanting to reinvent the wheel, in fact, I am trying to honour the wheel and carry its simplicity forward. The last thing I want to do is to teach anyone to 'suck spiritual eggs'. So, what am I getting at when I talk about building villages, finding connections and tapping into hidden intuitions? I get it, everyone knows how to say 'hello' to a stranger on the street. But this is merely an example to demonstrate what's at the core of a fragmented social culture.

It's about digging deeper. Being curious with what we find. Question more, and settle less. Whether we are wanting to discover a new community or trust our intuition openly, it's all about a willingness to do the work.

We have buried, filtered, programmed, edited and airbrushed so much that we have lost 'our hunter-gather' instincts. Some 2.5 million years ago, the caveman existed. And while progression is key, so many of our primal instincts have been lost. Emails, online chat rooms and social networking sites may have given us access to anyone in the world, but we have stopped relying on how powerful we were before the technological revolution. Whether you're on the hunt for a new friend, or a place where you belong, Circle and besties are not that different!

Next time you need an answer, I challenge you to search your inner-interweb. You'll be surprised at how clever your own Search Engine Optimisation (SEO) is.

Competitiveness in any industry can be rife but in a career where body size and looks can be a deal-breaker, my anxiety was through the roof. In some cases, women can fear women. Have you ever heard your female friends say, 'I am more comfortable around male energy?'

On many occasions, this can simply come down to shared interests. But it can also be a sign of genuine intimidation, fear of judgement and how we stack up against our peers. This fear has not been helped by social media, and false perceptions of what an independent and strong woman should look and act like. In fact, a strong and independent woman is more at risk of losing herself, because true vulnerability has become complex and seen as weak.

My request to you: Let's not allow fear to be the blockade between us, at a time we are craving connection more than ever. I think we are all searching for something we cannot create on our own. As a Circle Facilitator, I have witnessed first-hand, the power of trusting a woman, sitting shoulder to shoulder, tears to smiles, and loss to discovery.

Throughout my life, I have craved Circle and through adversity, I found it.

❍ A MOMENT FOR WISDOM

Hungry for … something

From a young age, I was craving something I couldn't put my finger on. I knew I was in desperate need of self-acceptance and belonging but I didn't know where, or how to find it.

My mother was consciously healthy and someone who worked out daily. She doesn't have a calorie counter but she is an advocate when it comes to taking good care of our vessel. Early on, I learnt the insider hacks on how to keep my body lean, with a fitness and eating regime that wouldn't waiver, for anything. However, I wasn't gripped by my eating disorder as a teenager – that came later. From dabbling with eating disorders, to an eight-year relationship with a Lebanese Muslim, as a young woman, I went from comparing myself with other women, to immersing myself in a community where women completely supported each other.

One evening, when I was preparing dinner with my then boyfriend's family, I stood there setting the table and overheard the women sharing among themselves. They talked of life, loss, grief and love. I thought to myself, 'Why is this the first time I am experiencing this? Why have we stopped, or never even started talking as women to women?'

The modern-day family dinner has become a thing of the past, replaced by solo dining and using devices for company. I'm the first woman to believe a woman's role is not just in the kitchen. But I learnt from my Lebanese sisterhood, that creating meals together, working as one, and talking over a chopping board allows space to talk. We would prepare meals together, and talk about miscarriage, death and financial struggles.

Circle is not a progressive way of living. It is an inbuilt artform that has been lost in history. And there is space for a comeback!

chapter eight

GOING DEEPER TO FIND CONNECTION

Let me tell you – when you know, you know. When people hear about Circle, I often get asked, 'Is it religious?' I know a lot of clichés spring to mind and it's easy to think, 'That's not for me!'

I can reassuringly say, no we are not religious based. Some Circle Facilitators, including myself, recognise a power greater than ourselves, but this power can go unnamed and also unrecognised if that is what is right for the Circle, the time and the space. How you show up in Circle is totally up to you – this is a place for people of all religions and atheists too. I have sat in hundreds of Circles and have no idea what the religious beliefs of most of the women there are.

There are many different shades of women in life, and we all have unique experiences. Circle welcomes hippies and CEOs, mothers and those without children. The importance of Circle is to acknowledge the broad spectrum of stories with empathy, openness, and willingness to listen.

What it does require is an open mind and an open heart. Follow these three steps to break down your barriers before we go on:

Step One: Find a spot that feels comfortable to stand on. This could be a patch of grass, your favourite rug or simply at a place you feel safe.

Step Two: Close your eyes and take some time to slow down your breath. Listen to the sounds around you; the birds in the background, the wind as it hits the trees and the noises that have become the soundtrack to your day.

Step Three: Slowly start to inhale, counting 1, 2, 3 and 4. Exhale to the count of 1, 2, 3 and 4. With each inhalation and exhalation, increase your count by a second. When you have reached a count of 10, repeat each round of breathing ten more times.

When you next feel like your fear is outrunning calm, get super still. We don't need to live in a future trauma that hasn't happened yet.

Breathe, and let the overwhelm pass.

❍ *The Love Drug*

The healthiest hit you will ever experience is 'the love drug', otherwise known as oxytocin, a hormone commonly associated with love, lust and labour. The infamous love drug is associated with childbirth, which acts as a pain-blocker and stimulant released to encourage contractions during labour.

Widely referred to as the love hormone, it sends a unique message to your brain which triggers protection, reduces postpartum bleeding and stimulates the production of breast milk. This hormone cleverly ignites the powerful feelings of love, the kind of love experienced when a mother holds her newborn for the first time.

But it doesn't stop there!

It is now largely understood that oxytocin has additional physiological pluses. Not only is the love drug released maternally, but we also feel this 'hormone hit' during intimacy with a partner, usually felt while hugging after sex.

The undeniable fact is that women have the power to generate and remedy life's harshest moments. Women have the knowledge and intuitive abilities to offer solace; to heal and create harmony all drawn from the strength of many gathered as one.

However, the strength and tenacity of women cannot be easily extinguished, and like-minded sisters have gathered in restaurants, quilting circles, church basements, mothers' groups and even the humble Tupperware party to tend with one another. Women still had the call to gather but neglected to delve into that energy that would diminish or overstate their inner power. But this power can be undoubtedly life-altering.

In these precious moments, we feel secure, content and wildly safe. With the human body being so intelligent, it is now believed that oxytocin is released as a stress response because it recognises threat. Under duress, the love drug encourages us to seek refuge, rescue and resolve – to tend and befriend.

❍ *Exercise: Look someone in the eyes*

Years ago, I went to a women's workshop, where we were tasked with the 'eye-gazing' activity. If you know what I'm talking about, you will know how insanely excruciating this can be.

We were asked to sit opposite another woman, usually a stranger, and for five uninterrupted minutes, we were instructed to look into each other's eyes. Sound simple? It is so hard! I can look into my dog's eyes all day long. But, on this occasion, ten seconds felt like an hour, and I had another 4 minutes and 50 seconds to go.

- First comes the internal questions: Did I leave the iron on? Did I send that email?
- Then comes the excruciating uncomfortable feeling that you have to face this moment and not escape it even though you want to run from it.
- Then comes the overwhelming need to cry. Why? Because our attempt at distraction is failing. We are being truly seen. With love and comfort.
- Then comes the letting go – the release and relief. Here is this stranger, accepting our raw beauty and lovingly

showing up for us. Yet, why can it be so hard to see our own worth and booming potential?

- I encourage you all to try eye-gazing with a friend or your partner. Sit together, set a timer and look into each other's eyes for five minutes (or try one minute at a time until you are able to work up to five minutes).
- If this feels too confronting for now, think about implementing the process into your everyday life. Notice how often you avoid making eye contact – with your friends, with your partner, with your boss, with the person serving your coffee.
- Make a conscious effort to look people in the eye – and really see them. It's the first step to really feeling seen yourself.

A close friend of mine in LA suffered from severe panic attacks. During one particularly bad episode, she called me. Hyperventilating and hysterical, she knew that she could trust me in her darkest moment. All that was asked of me was to just sit next to her. If she felt she was able to be touched, she would allow me to hold her hand, and I always asked permission first. I would wait for her to tell me what she needed. I was her village in those moments. Together we worked out how to make that possible, but only when she could open herself to it. In later years, she expressed how much this simple act of connection helped ground her so she could steady herself, when she was in the chaos of panic.

If you are not sure what your friend may need when struggling, ask them? We don't have to clear their tears or change the subject. We must allow our friendships to be free of guilt, burden and embarrassment. Everyone's needs are different and true connections strengthen when we are completely open to the unknown.

As humans, we like to think we are massively complex and, in parts, we are. However, we are also super simple. Strangers in a Circle are no different from our close friends if we see them as our equals.

Our village, Circle, or collective, are our survival kits. When tragedy strikes, don't run. Cook with your friends, walk with them, eat, paint or dance alongside them, sit in silence and trust that our resolutions require three things – us, trust and presence. And if you don't yet have a Circle of friends that will do this with you, my sister, you need to find a locally run Women's Circle and let it welcome you in.

'I've been called to Circle for a long time, and for a long time, I didn't listen. In 2020 I attended a Circle in a small country town in Victoria, Australia, and I loved it. At this time, the "calling" became stronger. Later that year I saw the Honouring Heart Circle Facilitator Training advertised on Facebook multiple times, like it was taunting me to do

the courageous thing and say, "Yes!" I fought it for a while, because I was worried that I wasn't good enough; that I wasn't enough of anything really and people wouldn't come. However, my strength came and in 2021, I began my Circle training.

'From day one, I felt like I'd come home. I loved the training and relished every activity, every learning moment and every bit of the training. I couldn't wait to get started each day. I learnt so much about myself; who I am. Deep down, I knew that I had so much to give and to offer as a Circle Facilitator.

'I now facilitate online Circles to clients globally. I am taking Circles home, to my little country town in Victoria, because this town is a part of me, my ancestry and legacy. I am alive when I sit in Circle and I feel the collective energy of those who have sat in Circle before me; my ancestors, my guides, my home.'

– *Shiralee*

chapter nine

QUIT COMPETITIVE SUFFERING

Have you ever started to tell a story, only to find mid-sentence, the person opposite starts to tell theirs? They say, 'I totally get it. There was this time ...', and before you know it, the roles have been reversed. You wanted to be listened to and now you're comforting them!

A lot of the time, it's done with good intentions.

If we hear that a friend is going through a rough patch, we want to show our solidarity and we do it by showing that we've also been there – or we were in a worse situation. We think that if we share something that is worse that has happened to ourselves, it may make the other person feel better.

Sometimes it does work but sometimes it doesn't – especially if our friends don't get a chance to feel seen or heard.

Here's the thing – unless we request permission to interpret their free-flowing brain dump, we are blocking their process to healing. They are now supporting us and our story, and their pain remains an open wound.

Any kind of competition stunts the power and process of Circle and that includes competitive suffering. So, how can we show our solidarity and share our own experience, without stifling each other?

Overshadowing a story is not always hogging the traumatic limelight but a way for us to say, 'You're not alone.' When I have been called on to offer support, I set the scene for safe sharing. I offer my friend permissions. These permissions can be anything including, for example: Can I share a similar experience? Do you want me to hold your hand? Do you in fact want any advice at all?

I will touch on this a little later. But at the crux of support, is knowing what *type* of support a person needs. There are rarely one-size-fits-all remedies during hard times.

chapter ten

YOUR SELF-ESTEEM NEEDS HUGS

I have a hard confession to share with you. I don't always practise what I preach.

I am a super-honest human and not a superwoman. My internal dialogue sounds something a little like this: *My daughter needs me; my husband needs me; the dog who suffers from anxiety needs me too.*

We are taught from an early age that the mother comes last, because the household needs her first. In our household, my husband and I share the load completely. However, when my daughter started teething and was not sleeping, I still found myself in a mindset of martyrdom and always putting myself last.Despite going unshowered, I am regularly posting on my business social media accounts, offering comfort to my friends and fellow mums, while writing this book. I am counselling friends and holding other people together, while I feel like I'm falling apart myself. I am definitely not, metaphorically, putting on my own oxygen mask first! Sometimes, I give more to the outside world than I give to myself. It's not uncommon for those who advocate for a healthy lifestyle, to be a little rusty in the self-care department. After all, we are all human. But, it's all about checking in with consciousness, kindness, and to really 'practise what we preach'.

Because I have spent years working on my self-worth struggles, I know that this has to swiftly change.

They say it a lot in yoga class: 'If you don't care for and love yourself, you cannot nurture those around you.'

We all have a scary tendency to do ourselves a disservice by not seeing our self-worth in the moments we need it the most. Bigging ourselves up daily is not a one-woman job, but it does start with us – it has to.

❍ *Your two-minute makeover to a softer start*

- Call a friend as you are boiling the kettle first thing. Explain your time is precious, but you just need to hear their voice.
- Set a timer on your phone (perhaps before you leave for work) for two minutes and just close your eyes, relax your facial muscles and breathe.
- This time is for you. It may not be a lot but it's amazing how grateful your self-esteem will be for a power-hug.

❍ *Real connection takes practice*

Sometimes, real connection is scary. I get it. It's confronting when we allow ourselves to be truly seen. But, we are only afraid because we don't get to do it enough. With so much of our lives happening instantly and digitally, in-person interactions are becoming a thing of the past.

When we intentionally find a safe space we can truly practise how to form real and authentic connections – with our friendships and in Circle. The 'tend and befriend' theory doesn't happen overnight. Forming trusted networks when we need them the most, is a process requiring trust and practice. When strangers become our greatest support systems, the stages of connection can be more subtle and simple than you think.

When I met a friend at an acting class in LA, I knew we were going to be close, but I wasn't prepared for the depth a friendship could go. At the time, I was exploring female relationships after spending years feeling threatened by them. I wanted to learn how to trust both in and outside of competitive cultures.

One day out of the blue, she asked me to go to a therapy session with her. Sure, we are used to hearing parents and partners joining their loved ones on the therapy sofa, but rarely, if ever, do we see friends going together. She told me that she wanted to discuss how we could discover complete female trust. It was magical.

We were both able to share our needs and boundaries. And we both needed to say, 'We are afraid of what happens if I let myself completely surrender to this trusting and female friendship.'

❍ *Nurturing your self-esteem in relationships*

Everything Circle is teaching me is that we must be open, honest and kind – especially about what's *not* OK. Being the social species that we are, means we hunt out those just like 'us'. It's not always easy. While I love my husband, Robb, very much, at times our marriage has truly been tested. But it's what's within these tests that makes us stronger, every day – even now, years on!

When times get tough, living in close quarters with a loved one can test a relationship's superpower. Sometimes, cohabiting during a rough patch or seasons of utter disconnection, can leave us craving some helpful tips on how to weather stormy waters.

Explain what you are feeling: We know that sharing our feelings is not always the easiest, especially in tension. We can often fall into the blame game, so using 'I' statements over 'you' can lower the defences. Clear your thoughts, and explain to your partner how you are feeling, calmly.

Work on the worries: If you are finding yourself going down an anxiety rabbit hole, it can be hard to see the wood for the trees. Mounting pressures, such as financial worries, can take a toll on any relationship, healthy or not. So, list your concerns and identify where the source of the worry is coming from.

Circle out of an argument: Have you ever been in a never-ending argument, or disagreement with no end point in sight? Whether it's because our ego needs to settle the score, or you are really that hurt, repeating arguments can become a merry-go-round. Say your piece, apologise for your part, and break the argumentative pattern by introducing the stillness that Circle has to offer.

Dig into the love: You love your partner, right? Sure, we can all get complacent, or forget our very own love story. Remember and see all the qualities you love about your partner. Scroll through your camera roll to happy selfies, and tender times. You both deserve that mutual joy.

Someone asked me recently, 'Do you ever get angry?'

Absolutely. I am human after all. But how I deal with it now is different from how the hot-headed twenty-something would have. A previous partner of mine recognised 'simmering under the surface rage' in me once. I have never equated myself as an angry person, but passive-aggressive, hmmm, sometimes. Dampening passive-aggressive tendencies as a mother and wife is something I'm becoming very aware of. Sleep deprivation as a new mother highlighted this trait of mine in my current relationship, and I am daily and consciously working on how to transform niggles into niceness. My husband and I have both gone through the rollercoaster of mental health hang-ups and that is strangely bringing us so much closer.

So, I keep coming back to three calm and basic techniques:

Practise stillness.
Breathe.
And … and ZIP it.

You can be near someone's anger but whatever you do, don't engage in it. You can acknowledge it. Allowing the person to have their moment, provided that they are not being abusive, will offer them space to defuse. Be grounded and connected to the earth. Be still. Circle is about providing space for every emotion, not just the ones less aggravated or frantic. Being in a Women's Circle gently allows us to share these healing and harmonising tips, that we can then take home to our families and friends. Being in Circle makes us better partners, mothers, CEOs and co-workers, and more importantly, helps us find our best selves to deal with the ever changing world. I can honestly say that Circle has helped me tame my anger. I feel much less reactive overall, and I believe it's because I intentionally take Circle as a gift for myself and a place to slow down my mind. It helps me to see all of my life more clearly, the beauty, the chaos, the light and the darkness.

'I had always been passionate about women's health and well-being, and I knew I wanted to do something within the wellness space but couldn't put my finger on what it was exactly. Until I went to a Women's Circle. I left the Circle feeling so well rested and I truly felt that I had done something nourishing ... just for me. That was a rare feeling as a mum of young kids. I left knowing that more women, and mothers, needed this in their lives. So I decided to delve further into facilitation and completed Imogen Bailey's training. I now provide a beautiful space every month for women to come to give back to themselves for a couple of uninterrupted hours. I run some Circles just for mums, and others for all women at any ages and stages of life. I create the centre of the Circle with care and intention, ensuring the room feels special from the moment women walk through the door. It brings me so much joy to be able to provide such a beautiful experience for these women, and a space they can come to in order to reflect, rest, recharge and nourish themselves from the inside out, as they so deserve.'

– Leah

chapter eleven

UNTAME YOUR INNER SIREN

The Siren, in Greek mythology, is a half-bird and half-woman creature who lured sailors to destruction by the sweetness of her song. The Siren is a temptress, a seducer and alluringly mysterious. Although the Siren is a mythical creature, there is something in her I absolutely love. A Siren owns her beauty and worth. She doesn't hand it over, nor does she apologise for her curves and desirability. A Siren woman has been woven into stories around the human condition for years, symbolising and embracing feminine power and raw sexuality.

The Siren call can be ignited in all of us.

❍ *What's your Siren Personality?*

As most of us cannot easily jet away to a mythical landscape, unleashing your inner Siren can be a tad more subtle. In fact, our modern-day programming has asked us to be a little more of everything.

Whether you are a partner, a boardroom vixen or a stay-at-home mum, our daily demands have required us to take on multiple roles. We are now defining our roles faster and harder than ever before. However, somewhere in the mayhem, we have become out of touch with ourselves. It's so easy to fall into unhelpful patterns; picking up the kids, bathtimes, scrolling into social media rabbit holes, and circling in the same friendships or comparison addiction that drains our sense of self. Breaking the mould can be liberating, even if a little unfamiliar.

By discovering your inner Siren, you can escape the daily grind, be brave in your dreams, be wild and free, and still hit your work deadlines. Even if you have a long commute, and three kids under five years old, tapping into your inner Siren, can make the daily grind doable.

❍ *So, what Siren Personality are you?*

- **The Goddess Siren:** The Goddess Siren fulfils her dreams. You command a room, and attract the attention of both men and women. You assert your presence and stand tall, but you can be silent, unapologetically. In fact, you love silence. If you stand at the top of a corporate boardroom, holding the attention of your work team, you are nailing your inner Goddess with oomph.
- **The Conquering Siren:** The Conquering Siren doesn't race others; in fact she isn't in any race at all. You love to conquer, but not compete. You are ambitious and

unwavering in chasing your goals. You are confident and unstoppable. Perhaps there is a book in you to be written, a job that you've always dreamt of, or a hobby that has sat on the back burner. Whatever the ambition, it's yours for the taking.

- **The Companion Siren:** The Companion Siren fulfils her need to connect. You prefer to move in a set of two, rather than living a solo life. You love to be around people and become the perfect and loveable host. You do not like the attention on you. Are you the mother who is the first to arrange a Saturday morning brunch, or a partner who likes to dote? You are the unwavering friend that everyone wants to be around, and a social hostess with the mostess.
- **The Mother Siren:** The Mother Siren loves to nurture and be nurtured. Providing safety for others is your purpose. You protect at all costs. You are calm, analytical and never hot-headed. You are the mother lion who protects her children at all costs, the friend who never lets her pals down, and helping people in the darkest times, comes easily to you without a second thought.
- **The Sexual Siren:** The Sexual Siren is ultra-feminine. You know your prowess and do not apologise for the word 'desire'. You own your sexuality. You are sensual and empower other Sirens. You know how to allure people into your energy, and walk confidently wherever you go. You know your worth, beauty, and are the magnetic Siren that everyone wants to be.

This is by no means an overnight transformation. Rarely, is there a lightbulb moment that 'just happens'. Knowing where you sit is one thing, knowing where you aspire to be is another. Like any form of personal empowerment, self-enquiry is key. Start simple and allow your curiosity to run free. Here are a few ways to unlock your Siren style – where limitless freedom awaits.

Get clear in your mind: Before you bin your favourite loungewear for free-flowing flares, create a draft of who you are craving to set free. Are you wanting to rebrand your personal image, or are you exploring local yoga studios? The shift may be an entire life overhaul, or as subtle as a new look. You might not be yearning for a lifelong makeover but wanting to tweak parts of your life that have been pushed to the back of the line. Understand your needs first and declutter your mind so your goals are crystal clear.

Style-up softly: When we have simplified and shifted our mindsets, the urge to change everything lessens! There can be an inner impulse to wake up and say, 'everything has to change', when in fact, nothing immediately can. Less speed and more softness can be as powerful without abandoning the non-negotiables. We start to write our resignation letters, book hair appointments and script out our break-up conversation. But change needs a soft touch to avoid regret and any sudden (and irreversible) jolts. Set an intention, that in the next 30 days, I will do one thing just for me.

Live life on the wilder side: OK, so we have cautiously explored your Siren call. You are in tune with your goals, and what you want out of life. You've made some BIG changes, and you are seeing a side of life, unexplored until now. Perhaps, you have identified the routines that no longer work for you, or teased your way out of unfulfilling friendship Circles. You are nearing closer to your Siren self because you experience a form of happiness that feels so right. You can no longer wait to put her into action. This is where I offer you complete permission to go wild. I am not saying book a sky-dive (though, totally do this if it's on your bucket list) but make the first move in the life you want to create. This could be asking someone out on a first date, launching a blog as a new writer, telling your partner you are ready to start a family or dying your hair pink. Your life – your choice.

Speak your absolute truth: If you feel it, say it. Live unapologetically, without an explanation. Avoid disguising a bad day, be honest with your desires and allow yourself the time to uncover or rediscover your silent Siren.

I invite you to call in your inner Siren, and regardless of whether you are one type of Siren or a pinch of them all (because there are no rules), embrace her.

Release, surrender and write

Size of group: *2–20*
Time required: *15 mins*
Resources needed: *Writing and journalling materials*

How the activity works: *We are going to journal about three things we want to surrender and release. Life is often thought of and spoken of by poets and authors and artists as a journey of letting go. Perhaps that resonates for you and if it does perhaps we always have a little something to let go of. This activity asks those in Circle, to write three things down that we wish to surrender and then under those three things we will journal about why we want to release them from our life. Wait until all the participants have finished and ask if they wish to share.*

chapter twelve

HYPE UP YOUR HIPPIE

Have you ever sat in traffic on your commute home from work, swearing that one day you'll move to a commune and live off the land?

Have you felt the calling to swap your urban lifestyle for #vanlife? Have you ever dreamt of selling all your belongings and moving to a surf shack on the beach?

I suspect we are all craving our own version of 'hippie life' – rejecting the excesses of modern society for a simpler, more earthy existence. The word 'hippie' can be met with a lot of judgement. If we hint that we're a hippie, people make assumptions and decide that we are a certain type of person.

Can we really have one foot on the bare earth, and the other on a corporate ladder? Absolutely!

Sometimes I catch myself 'dampening down my deep', even though my spiritual practices are a big part of my road to happiness. I used to apologise for talking about anything that could be seen as too unconventional – meditation, mindful eating, Reiki and energy healing.

Sometimes in life, healing moments can come at us a little out of left field. We all have a formula of what works, and what doesn't. That's not to say, that we should strike out alternative ways to heal. For some, the idea of sitting in Circle, can be seen as a hippie experience. I would like you to not rule out (or in) the prospect of sitting in Circle, because of a looming fear of stereotypes.

Labels are limiting and I think we all need to put down our personal 'label-maker' and suss out who we truly are.

Join me in becoming or discovering your inner-hippie; as a proud, progressive, business-oriented, flower-power and rainbow-loving woman.

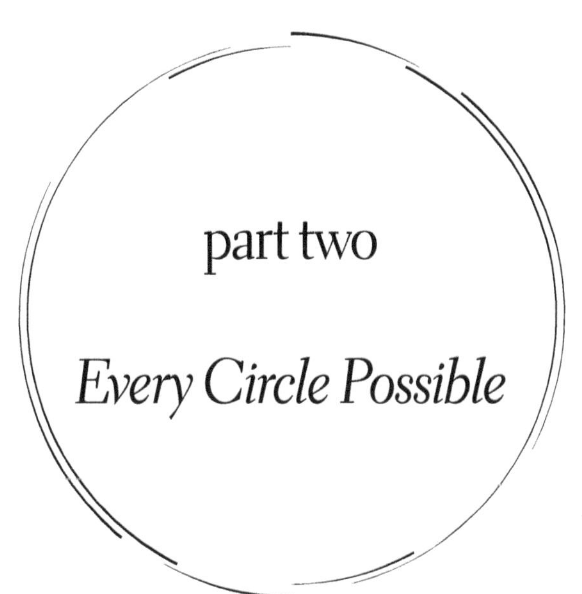

part two

Every Circle Possible

chapter thirteen

CIRCLE AS A CONDUIT FOR ENVISIONING

When we share our stories, we feel less alone

Can you recall the saying, 'a problem shared, is a problem halved'? Talking about a problem with someone else usually makes it seem less daunting or troubling. When we find the 'right' friend and courage to open up about a dark day, what is weighing us down suddenly becomes lighter.

We don't need to feel like a performer or a hero when we share our story. In fact, we can be anything but, however it can make us feel superhuman and empowered when we share our pain.

We can have a wobbly hand and a shaky voice as we share the parts of our story we consider to be our deepest secrets. Bravery comes the moment we choose to be vulnerable. And bravery is incredibly contagious – the more open we are, the more open people can be with us too.

Throughout the ages, storytelling has been ingrained in human nature. It is nothing new. For thousands of years, across cultures, religions and countries, there has been a very similar and sometimes unrecognisable formula. This formula is a little something like this: trauma + story + sharing = empathy, connection and oneness.

Conversely, storytelling has the power to heal. According to a study conducted by a group of neuroscientists at Princeton University,they discovered that when listening to a well-told story, the exact same areas of the brain light up on an MRI in both the storyteller and listener*. Your brain, as the listener, mirrors the brain of the storyteller. In simple terms, when you hear a well-told story, your brain reacts as if you are experiencing it yourself. Science has also taught us that the brain falls in love with a story, because when we hear a story, we are flooded with a release of hormones such as oxytocin and cortisol. Even now, as you read this book, you may feel comforted, understood, and will later communicate how you feel about what you are reading, to someone close by. The power of storytelling should never be underplayed.

Whether we are exchanging stories in a therapy group, a mothers' group, at yoga on the beach or in a support system for addiction dependency, they all rely on an openness that is rare in our day-to-day lives. Sure, we don't have

---

* https://www.ncbi.nlm.nih.gov/pmc/articles/PMC2922522/

to disclose our deepest beliefs to the barista in the local cafe but finding our own story corner has the ability to soothe our pasts, massively.

Following the global Covid pandemic, we felt the disconnect more than ever. Dr Annie Brewster, a health care professional working on the frontlines explained that, 'Storytelling is a balm for loneliness.' She went on to say, 'Storytelling is an inherently social practice, one that fosters intimacy and connection with others.'

Mental health sits at the core of storytelling, and by exchanging our truths, we can become the survival kit to someone else, and ourselves. We must stand by our pasts, experiences, talk as we would ordinarily talk, reflect without filters and protect the parts of our story that are not ready to be shared yet. If we consciously share and listen, limitless healing can happen and life can feel less lonely and isolated.

What is joy to you?

Size of group: *4–20*
Time required: *30–60 mins*
Resources needed: *a roll of art paper, various art materials including magazines and scissors for collaging*

How the activity works: *I encourage you to chat and get to know your Circle and the tradition of Women's Circle. This is how women would gather; to talk and make things, to weave and cook, but always to talk. Supply various art materials for your Circle and a roll of art paper (butcher's paper works). There are no real instructions for what you create, just that there is a vision for collective joy and whatever you channel, you put on the paper. Lay out a long roll of paper so that the women can be beside one another as they play. Put out various art materials and perhaps paint one big 'JOY IS' in the centre somewhere to get them started. Give them as much time as you feel is right to do this. The longer the better.*

Afterwards: *You may even choose to lead a meditation at the end after doing this activity.*

❍ A MOMENT FOR WISDOM

When our intuition is buried and why we must reclaim it

Unless you live in a meditative state 24/7, it's unlikely you will ever max out your intuition on a daily basis. In fact, we tend to mute our intuition in place for a safer, more predictable answer.

I can remember a turning point in my life where I put my intuition first, knowing it may end my successful career in media, music and entertainment. A publicist, unknowing that he was talking to a close friend of mine, uttered,

'Imogen Bailey is an example of a career that *could* have been amazing.' Ouch! But, at this point in my life, I'm OK with this.

In the early 2000s, I was asked to record a track with a renowned music producer in the UK. With my own personal entourage, I was flown over to England for a life-changing opportunity to hit the big time on the music scene. Quietly, I was terrified. My anxiety and social phobia was through the roof. I didn't know if I had what it would take to step up to the next level in stardom. One day, my courage was bursting at the seams, the next, I wasn't able to leave my hotel room.

I fought against the urges to jump on the next flight back to Australia and battled on. I made the record and went on to perform on stages across Japan and Europe. The track was mixed and played in the club scene and I was the next big star. The newspapers heralded me as the next 'Kylie Minogue', which as an Australian was a nice comparison (and aspiration), that I was more than happy to receive.

But, despite being offered a large sum of money, and on the brink of fame, I knew I wasn't able to maintain what was being asked of me.

One day, moments before I was meant to appear on stage, I froze. I couldn't go on and, on some level, I knew what I was doing. I was actively sabotaging the performance that would elevate my career. I knew I could no longer ignore what my intuition was telling me – that it was not the right step for me. I lost my record deal and my career in the industry was over, but my real work had only just begun.

I wish I had known sooner, that creativity, success and happiness existed in moments of contraction. That I was not weak but fiercely strong. For the first time in my life, I was listening to Imogen.

Why am I telling you this now? Because it all comes back to the concept of support. At that time, I was on tour – a lonely place to be. I didn't have my family or true friends around me – the people who would usually tell me the tough truths and support my gut feelings because they trust me.

When we find our village, we can tap into our intuition more easily because we feel safe and we know that, whatever we choose to do, the people who love us will support us. What's more, when we listen to our intuition, it's easier to accept and give support because we live from our true selves and don't need to hide.

'Practice listening to your intuition, your inner voice; ask questions; be curious; see what you see; hear what you hear; and then act upon what you know to be true. These intuitive powers were given to your soul at birth.'

– Dr Clarissa Pinkola Estés

❍ *Why our intuition is so important*

After losing the record deal and attempting to 'hit the bigtime' in the Hollywood hills, I returned to Australia once again determined to never ignore my intuition again. There was a huge part of me that still wanted to perform as a singer. But I knew if I did, I would still find myself in an industry that a person like me, perhaps wasn't designed for. For the first time in my life, I felt relaxed and at peace. I was determined to discover a path of service, purpose and meaning. Like most meaningful discoveries, none of this happens overnight. I knew I wanted to inject more kindness and connection into my life. I wanted Circle to become my life with all the pillars it stands for.

One decade on, after losing the record deal and meeting my husband, Robb, I said to him, 'It's time for me to let go of the career that has not served my heart and soul.' Ironically, as soon as I made that decision, I got offered a couple of great jobs, and yet, I turned them down. I created my business Honouring Heart, because I was honouring myself. And I want women globally to feel that they, too, can divert from any milestone if it means a truer and happier life.

The entertainment industry has a lot of pit-stops of self-worth proof points. It is an industry that acts as the biggest mirror to our silent struggles. Even nowadays, with a surge in social media comparisons, celebrities aren't as worshipped as they were before. People are not following influencers in the same way. Now, we are thinking about our own lives, milestones and meaningful moments.

To listen to your intuition is an incredibly intimate practice. As we become attuned to what really matters, there are fewer hiding places when it comes to the importance of listening to your heart.

chapter fourteen

CIRCLE FOR BIRTH

When I became pregnant with my daughter, the fears following recurrent miscarriages were suffocating. For any woman who has experienced this grief, I see you. Despite feeling ecstatic for the growing life inside of me, I was crippled with fear. Fear of the unknown and not knowing if I had the ability to cope with any further loss. Daily, I would call upon my support systems; my Circle for guidance. They became my Circle of mothers, all nurturing me during this time.

They didn't all have children (because that *really* didn't matter) but they knew how to use Circle as a nest of support and care.

As a mother-to-be, my Circle for birth sisters lovingly voted on roles to help me along on my journey. Some were tasked with organising my Baby Blessingway, or providing meals on the days where my high-risk pregnancy left me bedbound. This Circle was not just a display of loving friendships it was deeper than that. My trust and fragility was in their hands and I knew I was always so safe.

A Circle for birth is different and separate from gatherings like we see in a prenatal class. A Circle for birth is to protect the emotional journey as well as the physical. Some women choose to celebrate the Circle with dancing, belly decorations, and massaging the feet of the mother-to-be (a personal favourite ritual of mine). This type of Circle releases fears about birth and, as women we come together to honour and celebrate the mama-to-be, transitioning from maiden to mother.

Nowadays, mothers recognise that the 'standard birthing package' is not always enough. While the medical world exists to deliver a healthy baby with one hundred per cent commitment, a Circle for birth exists to provide one hundred and ten per cent commitment emotionally.

It is now, where I feel a responsibility to talk to the 'other' types of mothers. The mothers who have chosen to remain childfree, and those who sadly, are living childless; one is by choice, and the other is not. As we know, not every woman is able to carry a child biologically. Some choose alternative options, such as adoption or surrogacy to become a mother. It's a big and tricky topic to speak to; it's essentially a book itself. However, what I must say is this – mothers come in various forms. Some women are born unable, while others face the dooming reality of facing infertility without any notice at all. Women can mother in a multitude of ways. Some are teachers, healers, educators, aunties, sisters, daughters and people who want to care for another. We all might see motherhood through a different lens, and there is no wrong or right way to define this role. However, it is so incredibly important to say that a Circle for birth welcomes everyone. Whether you have a womb or not, a child or not, there is a space in your life (and soul) that has mothered, and is mothering. You are all so very welcome.

Becoming your version of a mother can be expansive, quirky and limitless.

chapter fifteen

SELF-LOVE – *the subject they need to teach at school*

There is nothing more heart-wrenching than overhearing a pre-teen or teenage girl whisper the words, 'I just want to be like the other girls.' This was said by a nine-year-old girl to my friend, her mother, who was starting to witness the early stages of an eating disorder take hold.

It crushes me to think of the road ahead, as she battles with self-acceptance in an age of social media.

No-one taught me what I needed to know. Craving belonging became a second-nature feeling. I wanted, needed, something different. I needed to find other women like me; wild women with a solid plan to grow. If you crave it, it's real and not indulgent.

Learning mathematical formulas and scientific theories at school is great, but my greatest ambition is to have fewer rows and more space for Circle in classrooms. There is no front or back of the classroom, but a space of equality and non-judgemental behaviour. The world needs leaders, I get that – but we also need unity. Gradually, we are seeing more 'Wellness Coordinators' on school faculties, but we have a long way to go.

❍ *To teach Circle is to teach love*

I want Circle to be a natural way of life, where stigmas of Circle are relinquished. Where people come to sample a 'taster' of healing and see what works for them. Sharing our thoughts and feelings can be embedded in a young person's mind, making openness acceptable. These skills can be morphed into all of life's formats: the family home, the workplace lunchroom, corporate programs, mothers' groups, yoga studios and lastly, within our dormant but yearning sisterhoods.

The 'Self-Worth Workout' is another subject I would add against algebra and textbooks. One of my favourite theories, 'The Bicep Theory', is all about emotional repetition to strengthen the negative thoughts against the positive. This theory is a workout for the soul. When we want to strengthen our muscles, we work on them, train them, nourish them, and sometimes, feel the pain in them. So, if we applied a regime to strengthen our mind, then the same theory could apply. It's all about growth, feeling the workout strain, and ultimately, becoming stronger. How long have we been working in the opposite direction?

Eventually, enough reps on the wrong belief system will come back and punch us in the face. I can't be any more unsubtle with that!

A dear friend and mentor of mine, Annie Swan, who is in her early 80s, often says, 'Imogen, it doesn't go away. The feelings of self-doubt and lack of worth will always be there. It is our job, as wild women and realists, to make self-love a daily practice.'

As a Circle Facilitator, I like to see those who sit in Circle, like a collective of wild flowers, in a beautiful garden. Like flowers, Circle needs nourishment, love and light in order to grow.

Joyful keepsakes and affirmations

Size of group: *2–20*
Time required: *15–40 mins (depending on size of group)*
Resources needed*: writing materials including paper*

How the activity works: *Most of us will be familiar with positive affirmations. Together in Circle, setting group affirmations will inspire joy and happiness. Ask everyone in Circle to create one, positive affirmation, before writing everyone's affirmations onto their pieces of paper. This affirmation may have been inspired by something a friend* *or relative of a Circle sister once said. There is no wrong or right when it comes to inspiring affirmations in Circle. Whatever is channelled from intuition, heart and imagination will be wonderful, I promise. What is created is an incredible list of co-created and powerful affirmations that are even more powerful because they have been created in the magic of Circle.*

chapter sixteen

CIRCLE FOR TEENS

When we bring teens together in Circle, they gain a richer understanding of how they are perceived by others beyond their physical appearance, and they can see themselves in a new light. Coming from a background in modelling, I know the dangers of comparison and competition. Our teens are being bombarded with physical comparisons 24/7 and they desperately need our support, guidance and open-minded understanding with what they face in a world obsessed with social media images. Circle helps young people feel nurtured and respected. It supports the exploration of self-love and compassion in a safe and often joyful environment. This work is incredibly rewarding, and, in many ways, this Circle contributes to our communities of young people searching for their identities.

❍ *Tapping into your 'inter-teen-tuition'*

So much of what we learn stems from our younger years, including our relationship with our body, our self-belief and our self-confidence. We know that eating disorders are on the rise in young people, as are the number of teenagers who experience depression and anxiety.

I was always a teen in need of belonging. When my parents divorced, we didn't discuss it, or heal as a family. This is one of the reasons I trained as a Teen Circle Facilitator. Your teenage years are the perfect time to begin to tap into the healing power of Circle. Why not start the Circle discovery as early as possible.

If I could say one thing to my 18-year-old self, it would be, 'Relax. You don't need all the answers today. If you are feeling uncomfortable, in competition and racing through your wins, please go slowly. You don't need to know it or have it all. Your intuition is your everything: arm it, trust it and protect it.'

We need to teach our children to share stories, experiences, troubles and big wins. Without it, we are aiding a culture of self-shaming, which can lead to depression and loneliness.

Myth: Circle isn't therapy. Talking isn't taboo.

Storytelling is educational. Storytelling is freedom.

lessons from circle

Leave your ego at the door

In Circle, we actively choose to leave our egos at the door. At times, we don't even share, let alone compare. Our traumas do not outdo the woman's sitting next to us. The size of her house is irrelevant. If she has a sleepless night, we don't offer her a night-time meditation tape.

Pay packets, followers, business deals and accolades are celebrated but not benchmarked.

Every woman is unique.

Here is a note I wrote to myself after one Circle:

'I must be open and transparent with myself and create a true dialogue with my inner critic.

'Reconnect and share with the woman who intimidates you.

'Ask with hands out, arms open: "Please embrace me."'

○ *Lessons from a Teen Circle Facilitator*

It is not as hard as you think to transform teen thinking! They are people too. Teens can be an intimidating demographic, but you don't need to be tech savvy or apply social media slang to communicate with them. To win teens over you don't have to try so hard – just talk to them like real people. And I have done my research, trust me. Teenagers need our help!

You don't need to reinvent the wheel: You don't need to create brand-new groups of youth. You could approach groups that already exist – like sports teams, youth groups and student councils. These existing groups may be open to adding a Teen Circle to their schedule.

Teens already sit in a classroom for six hours a day: Sitting and listening to a lecture is tough – even for adults. Show, don't tell – teens love hands-on, tangible activities that allow them to get up and move, think, communicate and share ideas. Which is all possible in a Circle format.

Teens might lack confidence: Shocking, right? Actually, a lot of teens assume they can't make a difference because they're told they are too young all the time to drive, to date, and do all the things that will mould them, not break them, the things they'd really like to do. They'll appreciate your vote of confidence.

They feel overwhelmed: You know that feeling when you watch the news and feel totally helpless towards whatever crisis is currently rocking the world? Yes, teenagers feel like that sometimes, too. If you give them the tools to change something, they'll feel like they actually can.

Teens like being the experts: Need help with something you don't understand, especially technology? Ask! Playing a vital role makes teenagers feel important and attached to a project. When they have done something 'not just anyone' can do, they feel unique and that deserves rewarding. They are our future leaders after all.

All is not lost: They might be part of a group, but that doesn't mean they personify it. Give them a chance to prove that they are more than their selfies suggest. Don't box them into a stereotype.

They smell your fear: Which turns them off, because they don't understand why they come across so scary. Relax and take a deep breath. They are a pretty forgiving crowd if they understand you're doing your best. Be confident and sincere, and you'll earn their respect.

Inspire them: Don't just give them your résumé; tell them short stories about how you got to your résumé. That will help you to gain their respect.

Give honest feedback: They're awesome lie detectors. There's nothing more patronising than when you say, 'Good job,' and walk away without a follow-up compliment. Maybe they're doing it wrong. Tell them. Failing, troubleshooting and fixing is a way of life. Teach them.

Let them play a part: If you let them brainstorm and make key decisions instead of simply giving directions, they will feel more invested and attached to the activity or project.

They might have a totally different worldview: And that's OK. They might have a completely off-the-wall idea on how to solve a problem. Short of anything likely to start a fire and/or get you in trouble, run with the craziness. It might seem improbable or impossible to you – but people said that about the aeroplane. Without new ideas, the world becomes stuck. Plus, if they have input, they take ownership.

Trust: They understand the ins and outs of more things than you would think of. Give them a proper environment and opportunity to thrive and they will deliver.

They respect and admire you for trying: They probably know you know more than they do. They probably just won't tell you.

'Back in my day': Avoid that phrase. No-one wants to hear that. Their day is now and current. Pass on your wisdom, but never assume it's the right fit for them.

Feed them: Teens are always hungry, and food helps them focus. This is especially true of teenage boys – who will always, always eat more than you think, or they say they will. A simple tip but a goodie. When sugar levels drop, you're going to wish you brought snacks.

Be goofy! Check your ego at the door, and they'll leave theirs behind too. If you're not willing to be at least a little silly at times, you probably shouldn't be working with teenagers. They do appreciate your lame humour – and it's probably not as lame as they lead you to believe.

One day, they will be you: And they will remember some of the things that came out of their mouths as teenagers and shudder. But right now, you're the only one in the room who has the benefit of seeing the situation through their eyes. Recall what it was like to be a teenager; awkward. Help them shape their identity, don't stifle it.

❍ *Teen Circle and the adolescent brain activity*

Let's create some ideas you can use in your programming for Teen Circles. It is important to always offer yourself some direction as a Circle Facilitator, by including purpose points for your Circle themes. These points can give you direction, focus and objectives to aim for. Some words I like to use for purpose points are, 'to define', 'to explore', 'to elicit', 'to examine' and 'to discuss'.

Here is a very effective example to help you form your Teen Circle activity:

1. Theme: Self care

The purpose:

1. To discuss what self-care is.
2. To explore the importance of self-care and how it feels to truly take great care of ourselves.

3. To define what activities and self-care practices each individual is called to for their own self-care.
4. To examine why it doesn't feel good when we don't take care of ourselves.
5. To elicit great self-care practices on an on-going basis and to teach Circle members that their practices may change as they change.

Additional themes may include: aspirations, community and what is important, family and friends, and lastly, confidence.

'The Teen Circle was next level awesome! The girls who joined us, totally blossomed and came into their own. Some of the girls said that they felt as though they had found somewhere they belonged. To feel empowered and more connected with my soul felt beautiful.'

– Teen Circle attendee

A Letter To You

I would like you to find a cosy corner to yourself. Make a cup of hot and comforting tea and turn your phone onto flight mode (if it's safe to do so). Take a few moments to reflect on the person you are now, and who you were on your 18th birthday. If you could travel back in time, what would you say to your younger self? What advice would you give her? What permissions would you offer her? What would you forgive? And most importantly, what would you celebrate?

At the top of the page, write the following letter prompt:

Dear 18-year-old self ... With love,

And once you've written your letter sign off from, 'Your future self x'.

You don't need to overanalyse or judge your words. Hold them, respect them and place them lovingly somewhere treasured and safe. And most importantly, honour that you are both the same incredible woman, with compassion and a few more life lessons under your belt.

Perhaps, try this activity at your home. I often use this self-enquiry exercise in Circle. There is something incredibly powerful about writing to your younger self. It offers comparison, reflection and insight.

❍ A MOMENT FOR WISDOM

Is your 'inner teenager' acting out?

Our teenage years can be a time of great loneliness when we really feel like we don't belong and, for many of us, that can leave a long-running wound that continues to affect us. Take some time to think back to your teenage years, such an important 'coming of age time' in girls and boys, becoming women and men.

What are your memories of your teenage years, especially when it comes to how connected you felt to friends, your family and your wider community?

When your loneliness is triggered, how does your inner teenager feel? This can impact how we talk about and also react to our loneliness.

We can be afraid to ask for help, regardless of what stage of life we are in. The 'Wise Woman' tends to be averse to reaching out and believe it's a weakness in themselves if they try. The young teenager (our inner teenager) may be incapable of identifying their emotions and understanding the meaning behind them, so becomes stoic and silent. The teen in us acts out, the wise withdraw.

Withdrawal and holding back can be a response that developed over years of having to do things for ourselves. It could also be the result of profound rejection. Fear of loneliness or isolation can be overcome if you reach out to other people in your life and share your concerns.

chapter seventeen

CIRCLE FOR WOMEN'S CYCLE

One better-known Circle is 'The Red Tent', and the symbolism of this Circle is mind-blowing! This ancient gathering is to symbolise and gather women in a red tent at the time of menstruation.

Derived from ancient Native American traditions, 'The Red Tent' honoured the time of menstruation with the 'Red Tent' ritual. Women would live in a separate lodge while menstruating, said to be synchronising their menstrual and lunar cycle together.

During this time, a woman was considered to be more creative and in tune with the spirit world. Within 'The Red Tent', away from the masculine roles, women were provided a safe and supportive environment where young women learnt about the responsibility of their fertility cycle and the importance of their role as women in tribes, culture and society.

A dear friend and former student of mine, Andrea Garcia, is now the President of Red Tent Australia. This incredible platform acts as a non-profit organisation with the aim to connect, collaborate and create a community of strong and educated women in a supportive environment.

They host established community networks and build support between women by hosting local gatherings and events in what they call 'Red Tents'. It's their hope for everyone who enters each Red Tent to experience a sense of belonging, sisterhood and strength that stays with them from then on.

According to Ann Landaas Smith, founder and director of Circle Connections, there are menstrual hut and 'Red Tent' moon lodge traditions all over the world that date back to 800 CE and in some places are still practised today. These are 'seen as sacred spaces for women and girls to affirm their spirituality and sexuality, and to heal from the wounds of patriarchy', she says.

Red Tent Circle Letters

'I wanted a deeper understanding of the effect of the lunar and seasonal cycles on my emotions, energy levels and psychological states. Attending Red Tent Circles for five years now, has taught me how to create balance in all three cycles, with a cyclic approach to self-care. It's been a fascinating awakening. I'm forever grateful.'

– Danielle

chapter eighteen

A PERSONAL STORY – *repairing self-worth after rejection*

From the age of 16, I was in a faithful (from my side), long-term relationship with my teen sweetheart. I was head over heels in adoration for this man. He was my first true experience of love, or so I thought. But, the love was a one-way street as I discovered that on multiple occasions, he had been unfaithful to me, leaving me with one unanswered question: 'Why am I not enough?'

If you have ever been cheated on, you will understand that this discovery can destroy your self-esteem. For the unfaithful party, it may be a frivolous, ego-stroking and sexual kick. For the cheated on, you will question everything about yourself: Am I not pretty enough, thin enough, engaging enough, successful enough?

Unfaithfulness has the ability to wound a person and this scar can be difficult to heal.

At that time I was 24 years old. I was broken-hearted, single and already at an age considered to be 'over the hill' in the modelling industry (I know, I know, my current self agrees that's crazy). I was determined to show my ex how worth it I was. On repeat, I thought, 'Damn you. I will show you that I am amazing. Just look at how many modelling agencies will sign me now.'

Inadvertently, and silently, I was screaming for validation. A polarising and starkly obvious choice to prove my worth which was at a crippling point.

I was rigid with calorie counting to the point I was diagnosed with the life-threatening eating disorder, anorexia nervosa. As a gym junkie and at the peak of my career, I would work out twice a day, and throw in an extra Bikram yoga class for good measure. Sweat and self-loathing were my friends.

Newsflash (not newsflash), the modelling and entertainment industry is incredibly competitive. Walking into castings, my anxiety was on high-alert. I was faced with seemingly flawless and fiercely determined women. Even now, I question a room when I walk into it: **'Am I in a safe place for my worth?'**

Thankfully, these days, the answer to that question is usually yes. I am in a safe place, because I choose the rooms that I walk into (metaphorically and literally). And you can too. Start to pay close attention to the people who make you feel comfortable, valuable, worthwhile and seen. Pay attention to the people who drain your energy and make you feel less than. Then tailor the time you spend with them accordingly.

If a job is draining you every single day and you've tried everything you can to change it, then leave it. Have faith in yourself to find a better option and value yourself enough to make that leap. In all this talk of loneliness, choose to be alone over being with the wrong type of people for you. This is especially true if you've been hurt, rejected or betrayed, when it's tempting to fill that void with anything or anyone.

That heartbreak in my early 20s led me into a modelling career that I can't regret, as it also led me here. But it also fed my insecurity and damaged my self-belief for a long time too. Don't give up on finding yourself, because healing others also starts with you.

Recently, after speaking with friends and Circle attendees, I've felt a collective emotional 'slump'. One by one, people have shared how social media feels like a front row seat to atrocity, political unrest, and suffering of those we don't know. While I am all for social media and multiple news channels sharing the headlines we need to be aware of, we are also flooded with negative unrest. We are seeing worldwide problems unfold that we cannot directly heal. We read how financially vulnerable the economy is or how world leaders are planning attacks on innocent civilians. It is impossible to not feel powerless and ... devastated.

In this unsafe world, Circle promises safety. It may not be able to sit in parliament or trade organisations, making executive decisions to cure the world. But, Circle is neutral. Circle is a temporary bunker away from fall-out. Circle is a cocoon. Circle doesn't claim to eradicate a crisis, because Circle is designed to feel all the feelings. However, Circle holds pain with peace and permission to let our modern-day guard down.

If we cannot heal a broken world, we can heal ourselves to live in it.

Acceptance through discovery

Acceptance ritual
Size of group: *4–20*
Time required: *15–30 mins*
Resources needed: *copies of the poem below and tea light candles*

How the activity works: *This is a ritual for calling in acceptance. Ask each Circle participant to take a copy of the 'wise woman' poem and a tea light candle.*

Prompt with this instruction:
'I ask that you sit in silence and contemplate that which you feel needs the most acceptance in your life. Place your hand on your heart, close your eyes and breathe deeply into your full self. Allow whatever needs to come up to

gently come up and when you have your thoughts and feelings gathered open your eyes to let me know that you are ready to begin.'

When all women are ready it's a lovely offering to share this poem with the Circle.

'I see the wise woman. And she sees me. She smiles from shrines in thousands of places. She is buried in the ground of every country. Everywhere I look, the wise woman looks back. And she smiles.'

– Susun Weed quoted in *Birthing Ourselves Into Being*

Acceptance can be a sticky and tricky emotion that can swell in these moments.

Afterwards: *it is important that you end this ritual with something elevating like dancing, singing a song, chanting or taking a walk in nature.*

❍ A MOMENT FOR WISDOM

Exposing Our Disconnect

You might think that nailing teenage life will set us in good stead to nail adulthood. However, how many times have you faced teenager feelings in an adult mind? Sure, as adults, we have the ability for greater self-awareness and have gained basic life tools to 'do life better', but, at times, I question how far we *really* have come in a disconnected world?

In 2008, at the peak of my career, I signed a three-year contract to appear on Australia's iconic soap opera, *Neighbours*. I was ecstatic. Until, out of the blue and only six months in, my character was axed and written out of the show. At the time, a new executive producer at *Neighbours* was being criticised for hiring too many models. Former Miss Australia Erin McNaught and I were dominating the press rounds and were constantly referred to as models and not actors. The producers were concerned that the audience wouldn't take the show seriously.

Tough? It was! However, it was also meant to be.

After my contract was cut short with *Neighbours*, just six months into the three-year contract, I didn't know what my next move would be. A year after I left *Neighbours*, I found myself in a long-distance relationship with an actor based in LA. We originally met when I went to LA for an overdue holiday, and also to suss out the acting scene that I hoped to break into. Although I didn't have any plans to move halfway across the world, it made sense to pack a bag, up-sticks and head to America.

I always remember how lonely Hollywood felt. I was surrounded by the broken dreams of actors who didn't make it. There was also a massive sense of success. But there was a sense of complete disconnection and loss.

The more I think about all the cities I have lived in, they all have one thing in common – unbelonging. There was no leaning over garden fences to say hello or borrowing a cup of sugar. How can we share a planet, but not say hello?

After that relationship ended and I found myself heartbroken and broke, Circle became my salvation. It also helped me to look behind the curtain of Hollywood. Guess what? When I started to attend an LA Circle Group, I saw very successful actors there. People who I thought had it all!

Like everyone, these successful actors who had made it to the big time, still knew something was missing. Connection, authenticity, a space where they didn't have to be perfect! A place like LA has two paths.

I chose the right one for me. To heal, to nurture, and to nourish.

chapter nineteen

CIRCLE FOR WEDDINGS

I was just as excited about my Bridal Circle, as I was about my wedding day. The purpose of a Bridal Circle is to create a ceremony that is bonding, fun and loving for the bride or couple (if they have a Wedding Circle) before they embark on their wedding day journey, which can often be stressful and as most brides and grooms will tell you, it will fly by! Bridal and Wedding Circles provide opportunities for all members of the wedding parties to lessen the nerves and minimise stress over to-do lists, and slow down and be present so the big day can be fully embraced.

I never had a hen's night or engagement party because this was different; I was different. This decision was driven by my absolute intention to celebrate love. I wanted to fill my home with women, ceremony and ritual. My big day was finally here, to be blessed and loved in my own Bridal Circle.

I invited my mother and my closest girlfriends who love, honour and elevate me. My grandmother sewed me a 'wedding quilt'. This quilt will go to my daughter, and perhaps it will go to hers (if she wants to pass it forward).

I highly recommend all women have a Bridal Circle, and it's not complicated to do so. Here's some simple steps to hold one for yourself or someone you love.

Go for home-made: Rather than buying presents, the women at my Circle made me gifts. This meant so much more to me than something they could Click-and-Collect.

Choose activities that connect you: We shared stories, meditated and journalled together. We also wrote poetry and chanted, although I understand if that's a little too far for you.

Make it all about the bride: When I sat in my 'Bridal Circle', I sat on a chair in the centre of the room and shared the story of how I met my husband, our first date and how we fell in love. Our joy became their joy.

Giving the gift of wisdom: Our lovely family and friends shared their stories too. Mirroring experiences provides empathy and comfort. Learning about how others navigated the course of love; how respect is a two-way exchange and how to continue honouring the union, was highly powerful. And enormously helpful.

Make it fun: Weddings can be stressful during a time when great expectations are placed on brides (and grooms) so please, encourage her to let her hair down! Support her to dance like a wild woman or participate in a deeply moving ritual. I encourage the ritual to be something unique that you create for her. Once, I had a friend who wanted her body painted in mud. Muddied up, we created a 'live fire centrepiece'. Scribbled onto pieces of paper, were her fears about marriage and the next steps she was about to take. With each movement, we threw those fears into the fire. She wasn't naked, but wearing an old dress from her adolescent days. For her, this ritual was about letting go of the crap and fears about marriage and commitment (AKA the mud and dirt). This was so immensely moving, but also very fun. In fact, we ended the evening in a friendly mud fight. We had a ball, teared up and laughed with joy. For this bride, it was a Circle memory that she has never forgotten.

Whether you choose to bathe the feet of the bride and groom, or dance around a fire, the most important thing to remember, is that this is the ultimate celebration of love.

We form relationships because love feels good, am I right? Celebrating all the people in our lives in Circle, honours that person and solidifies why they exist in our world in the first place. Certain activities should be fun, creative and light-hearted, but they should also bond the group.

Here is an example:

Have the bride and groom sit on two chairs in the centre of the Circle and have them tell stories about how they met, first dates and the moment they 'fell in love'. As a Circle Facilitator you will guide this activity, by asking questions, allowing them to fill in the heartfelt 'blanks'. You can also ask the parents, grandparents and friends of the happy couple, to share their pearls of wisdom for a happy marriage.

After all, every love story is worth savouring.

Another beautiful Circle offering with a twist, is the Bridal and Wedding Circle. The purpose of the Bridal and Wedding Circle is to empower and honour the bride, or to offer a fun bonding ceremony for the bride and groom as a true gift. The difference between a Bridal Circle and a Wedding Circle, is that a Wedding Circle is for both the bride and groom, alongside their dearest friends. The opening and closing ceremonies differ in that for a Bridal Circle, the focus is all on our bride and the activities are all about creating gifts and blessings for her.

The Wedding Circle is a Circle that creates a type of ceremony, that is bonding, fun and loving for the couple before they embark on their wedding day journey. Often this can be a stressful time, and inevitably time passes so quickly, that celebrating the engagement can be overlooked! The Wedding Circle is an opportunity for the bride, groom and wedding party to slow down and be present inside the love story and special day. We open and close this

Circle just as we would a Women's Circle but we change our words to offer personalised blessings to the couple.

For a Wedding Circle the opening and closing ceremony is a blessing for the couple and their wedding as they embark on their beautiful journey together. Entering this next chapter of life is an incredibly sacred and significant rite of passage for a woman.

Gathering with sisters to honour, bless and support the bride-to-be is a beautiful and meaningful ceremony, which will stay in her heart forever.

❍ A MOMENT FOR WISDOM

A different type of love

My husband, Robb, and I have been married for eight years. We got engaged during our first year together. We were madly in love with one another and it felt beautifully wild. However, unlike my previous long-term relationships, I knew instantly that this was a love I could totally trust. Because I finally trusted my senses, intuition and I was the woman I was always destined to become. Only then was I ever truly prepared to meet my person. Only then, did I trust that my inner voice was the only voice I needed. I didn't need outside advice, relationship columnists or fantasy love stories to show me I was all I needed to be and that Robb was all that I wanted from love.

I took a job as a waitress in a local restaurant shortly after filming finished on a TV hit, *Go Back To Where You*

Came From. I needed a break from TV and modelling work. I was craving anonymity and normality. I also needed a steady income to support my study in becoming a doula.

Robb would regularly come into the restaurant for coffee or the occasional dinner with friends. While I thought he was a good-looking guy, I wasn't looking at him in *that* way. Not instantly anyway. We would always have 'big chats' about the meaning of life, our struggles and hopes for the future. It was refreshing to meet someone who I could really talk to, where I was heard too.

Robb had a successful career in business development, and always appeared from the outside, to have it all. He was charming, polite, funny and intelligent. I love these qualities in a person, but with Robb, something else opened my eyes to the incredible man he was. During one of many conversations, Robb disclosed to me that he had battled and survived bowel cancer.

Like me, after experiencing so much loss and displacement, he too was searching for answers and a deeper meaning in life. He also had no idea who I was, which was both refreshing and a relief. I loved that I was a nobody, who could be his somebody one day.

At the time, I used to go for a run every day on the same running route. I remember, one day, spotting one jigsaw piece underneath a tree, which seemed strange. I stopped to see if I could find any stray pieces.

Not far from this tree, was a car with a registration plate which read: Rob. I had been looking for a sign and it seemed like this was it.

I later learnt that his house was opposite this tree with the single puzzle piece and the car spelling out his name (it didn't belong to him).

At this point in my life, I actually loved being single. Being alone and free to find out who 'Imogen' really was, and wanted to be, felt right. I was understanding what I wanted versus what I needed. I didn't need a man in my life, but I wanted to remain open to love. I wanted to be a team with Robb. He wanted to see the woman who loved to chant at dawn. He would often say that I intrigued him and he was curious about how Circle became part of my life. So much so, that Robb has now become a fully-fledged Circle Facilitator too. There is zero competition between us, only encouragement.

When I accepted Robb's hand in marriage, I knew that he was exactly the person I was supposed to meet. I knew that he was my person, the person who would become the father of my daughter and the person who I could grow old and happy with.

Today, I run my company Honouring Heart with Robb right by my side. He is doing incredibly important work in running Men's Circle. Robb offers a perspective that I as a woman do not have. In recent years, Robb has created, carved and developed programs perfectly fitting for men. We brainstorm together on the whiteboard sitting in our living room. We heal together and blend what we know about Circle into our everyday life.

Today, our lives are totally intertwined – our work, our family, our social circle – and I'm OK with that. For someone who was so independent, I am so grateful to have softened and really let him in.

chapter twenty

MY INSIGHTS – *as a doula, I am the witness to the journey of the soul*

When I became a birth and end-of-life doula, I realised that one thing stood out, that stillness heals the absolute unknown. Becoming a doula, while a 'career' choice, was and is a great privilege. To observe, witness, and be part of such milestone moments in a person's life, is nothing short of an honour. I have seen the first and last breaths taken from those entering and leaving this earth. This is the journey of the soul. And something that can be seen and felt while sitting in Circle.

I have learnt how to embrace love and fear, and to listen rather than trying to fix.

We have this need as humans, to fill silence. However, we don't always have to say something. Be present. Be there. Be fearless. Speak from your heart and the ancient wise person that lives deep within us all. Sometimes I just hold the hands of those who are meeting grief; I look them in the eye, and ask, 'What do you want to say?' When you don't know what to say it might be because you are being presented with a moment to just listen.

❍ *Becoming a doula of your own making*

Obviously, not everyone has a calling to become a birth or end-of-life doula. Sometimes, there is a simpler way to introduce 'manifestation' into our lives without becoming a support system for mothers-to-be, or the terminally ill. It can all come down to a big (but simply put) question: What is it we want from our lives?

It was only when I asked myself this question, that I knew a love story was heading my way.

When I met my now husband, Robb, in the local restaurant where I was waiting tables, we had an instant connection that was special.. We were both on similar paths. Robb had undergone his own self-discovery and was open with his feelings – I loved that. I still do, immensely.

I am not going to lie – I totally manifested Robb via my vision board. Perfectly positioned on this board was the letter 'R' and the number '7'.

I cannot pinpoint the exact moment I introduced manifestation into my life. The power of manifestation feels like a deep knowing and can act as an invisible guide forward. To tap into vibrant, colourful and emotive visions (yes even a smell), is a way of trusting something that the naked eye cannot see.

In my teens, I discovered a passion for vision boards; a collection of images or objects arranged in a way to help you manifest your goals or vision. A vision board acts as a spiritual compass and 'wish-list' for our future.

At first, I would use my bedroom wall as my 'wish-list' canvas. I would tear colours, pictures and words from magazines and place them on my bedroom wall. This wall became my inspiration. It was both an exciting and natural process.

In my 20s I began to see certain elements of my vision board appear in my life. These occurrences wouldn't always be exact replicas, but a twist on a symbol or sign, showing me that I was on the 'right' path.

I am a ritual woman at my core. I use ritual in my life to call in what I want, and to surrender what I no longer need. When I reached the chapter in my life where I knew I was ready for true love, I knew the starting point was my trusted companion, the vision board. Though I was no longer using my bedroom wall, I found the perfect cork canvas to create my 'love' wish on.

Vision boards are very powerful and now very popular tools. Even the top life coaches in the world like Anthony Robbins, Jay Shetty and Gabrielle Bernstein encourage us to use them.

The board to manifest my husband took months to perfect.

I started with finding words, letters, numbers, images and poetry that inspired me. I began to visualise my future partner as though he had already arrived. I allowed my intuition to guide me. This is also another reason why I love Women's Circle, because intuition is completely embraced.

My vision for Robb (my husband), featured a prominent number '7' and the letter R on it. At the time, my analytical brain wasn't certain why this number was so special, but my heart knew. After all, seven is my number. I was born on the seventh of the seventh, in 1977, seven minutes past seventeen hundred hours.

However, when I chose this number for my vision board, it seemed to be coming from something, or someone, else. I now know it was coming from my husband.

Then came the letter 'R'.

I was powerfully pulled to place the letter 'R' in the centre of my vision board. I had no idea why at the time, but it felt completely right. When I met Robb, the universal penny dropped, and I was blown away. He was my big R and my number seven; he was born on 7 February, and has a Roman numeral 'VII' tattooed on his ribs on his 'right' side. He is everything I lovingly placed on that board and more.

Creating a vision board is super personal. I created the board slowly, with support from my other spiritual practices, helping me access my creativity and complete openness. I made my favourite tea, I meditated, I contemplated in silence, I danced and felt deeply into each item placed with love on the board. It might all sound a little wild but don't knock it until you try it. Maybe you have something or someone you want to call in and maybe reading about this process is your sign?

The next part of the vision board process is placing it somewhere your eyes will be constantly drawn to. With this particular board, I took things a step further and every time I saw the board and my vision, I would say either aloud or in my head, 'Thank you. Thank you for bringing my visions to me.'

I was always saying 'YES!' to Robb before I met him.

This, I believe, is a huge key in manifestation. Follow your intuition and decide what you want and keep saying yes with passion until what you want appears.

A 5-step vision board

1. *Talk to your intuitive voice and your heart and tell it you are ready to listen.*
2. *Decide what you want to call in and reflect on your wishes until they feel clear.*
3. *Find images, words and items that inspire you (remember to follow your intuition and use rituals that feel right to you).*
4. *Create an emotive collage on a board (or wall if it calls you).*

5. *Display your board in a prominent place and keep saying yes and thank you to your vision until it manifests into your now.*

If you believe vision boards are a little 'woo-woo', that's OK, but for me, I called for love and she delivered in spades.

Refreshingly, Robb wasn't and isn't afraid to have the hard conversations. We have been together for ten years and married for eight. It was during these hard conversations that we uncovered our joint desire to become parents.

I was 39 years old the day we got married, and as Robb sensitively put it, 'We aren't getting any younger.' My biological clock was chiming and, with a family of fertile genes, the prospect of falling pregnant quickly, was a given.

Although falling pregnant was easy, loss was not.

Loss

I cannot carry you,
Though I don't want to let you go.

Together we surrender,
My body,
Your body.
We let each other go.

Swimming in the genius of nature.

Hearts floating in the unknown

There is sadness
There is love

There is faith

This is all I know, Miscarriage.

Imogen x

activity

Intuitive love art collections

Size of group: *4–20*
Time required: *30 mins (longer if bigger group)*
Resources needed: *various art materials including large sketch paper and music to play while Circle participants are working*

How the activity works: *Provide art materials and ask those in Circle to take materials of their choice and partner up. First, partners will face each other for one minute. Prompt them to look into each other's eyes and then after one minute take a pencil or pen and some paper and, with eyes closed, draw the other person from memory. Often these drawings are like a child's drawing,* *and how fabulous is that! How often do we look into each other's eyes and then let ourselves express ourselves blindly? This is intuitive love art and the perfect gift for Circle partners.*

chapter twenty-one

CIRCLE FOR MEN – *let's bring back the brotherhood*

Without stating the obvious, I am a lover of Women's Circle … because I am an abundant woman. I am drawn to the feminine energy that is embedded in a collective of women. But that's not to say that men are not drawn to the same principles of Circle either. In fact, some of my closest friends and favourite Circle Facilitators are men who have healed themselves through a yearning to connect with other people.

Sadly, we know there is still a stigma that stops men talking openly about mental health struggles. For generations, fathers and grandfathers have lived by the notion, let's say rule, that 'boys don't cry'. For many, there is a dangerous belief that if you show emotions, you are weak.

I'm passionate about both understanding and teaching the ancient lineages of gender roles; men hunt and gather, women, nest and nurture. Despite my overwhelming joy to honour these roles, I also need to say, it doesn't always work for the greater good.

This isn't a new topic. Social media and mainstream news often refer to the silent killer among men – suicide. According to Lifeline Australia, the suicide statistics are startling. Nine Australians die every day by suicide. That's more than double the road toll. Staggeringly, 75 percent of those who take their life are male. These facts speak for themselves.

The good news is, a change is happening. Incredible male-founded organisations like Movember, One Wave is All it Takes, and Hello Sunday Morning are bringing people together to talk openly about our emotions, no matter what gender you identify with.

We need to be flexible with our viewpoints in light of our present day. The world is changing, and we need to change with it. This is where equality comes in. I don't mean professional equality or challenging the gender pay gaps, but an equality in spirit, heart and emotions.

Despite fully immersing myself with my fellow brothers in Circle, I will never truly understand the burden that many men feel to hide their pain. That's why I decided not to write this chapter myself. Instead, I wanted to pass it to my husband, Robb, a Circle Facilitator who has worked with me to grow our company, Honouring Heart, from the beginning.

I encourage you to pass this chapter to the men in your life, who could benefit from genuine connections.

❍ *It's not cool to be a man with feelings*

My name is Robb, a Sydney–born and bred suburban Aussie. I played sports like most and was a bright kid, who got bullied a lot for being, well, bright.

During high school, my academic ability landed me in classes designed for kids who excelled above the rest. Now, being an intelligent teen is actually not that cool. So, I pretended to be dumb to avoid a kicking.

I'm not the only man who has downplayed their ability to fit in with a crowd. It's common for men, starting when we are boys, to change our personalities and our preferences to belong – first at school, then in our personal lives too.

When I was 19, I dropped out of university, partway through studying a Bachelor's Degree in Psychology. Studying was not for me, or so I believed. Partying was. So, I moved to New Zealand, scored a few bar jobs and taught snowboarding. Life was good! However, I already had a craving for a deeper connection.

In some ways, despite my hedonistic lifestyle, I realised something back then – I wasn't just a man who could get on with virtually anyone from any walk of life. I was drawn to the harder conversations in life. It's the one natural skill set I am very proud of: I can get into extremely uncomfortable conversations with people and, at the end of them, I'm invited for Christmas dinner!

Something inside of me has the ability to step into an emotionally charged space and defuse the energy to a feeling of safety. What I've discovered since then, in my work with Circle, is we ALL have that ability – the ability to neutralise a conversation; to harness sadness and fear. But, it's an emotional muscle we have forgotten how to use.

So often I hear: 'Men aren't good at emotional conversations.' But, I've had incredible conversations with men throughout my life, when they are given permission to talk openly, honestly and authentically.

You don't have to join a Circle to do it but, for many men, a safe Circle can offer them a place where they feel they have the permission to speak freely. A circle can really be a healthy space to practise talking more and allowing the words to flow freely. That is a gift for all.

❍ *Great businesses are built on curiosity and connection*

At just 25 years old, and two weeks before I was due to start a dream job in the advertising industry, I got a phone call that changed my life. 'Robb, you have bowel cancer.' Nothing, and I mean absolutely nothing, prepares you for that kind of news. I called my new employers and asked if I could postpone my start date by six months. Their reply? 'Robb, you must be dreaming. There are a hundred men waiting to get this job. I'm sorry, but the job offer is off the table.'

After six months of chemotherapy, half my intestine removed and weighing just 58 kilos, I was at the darkest point of my life. Every day, I would lie on the sofa gaunt, thin and broken. All I kept asking myself was, 'Robb, what the hell are you going to do with your life?' I was in the deepest, thickest and most earth-shaking depression. And I didn't know how I was going to get out of it.

At the time I was single (this was eight years before I met Imogen). With little energy, friends or hope, I still somehow held on to my curious spirit. I lost myself in teaching myself new skills: everything from self-help to web development and design. As a creative, getting lost in my imagination was a form of escape.

Fast-forward to the present day, and I can see that those dark times led to me finding my passion. I've run multiple businesses, and formed multiple partnerships, because I lived through that traumatic experience. It taught me, not only business skills, but how to be resilient, agile and treat other people with compassion.

In the first few months of our relationship, Imogen would tell me about all the plans she had to make Circle a global movement. And I was in! But, to me, Circle looks a little different …

❍ *Newsflash: men gather in Circle*

The Women's Circle is a pretty cool concept. I don't have the words that Imogen does, but I do see the power of connection. Together we run Circle for men and women, sometimes separately and sometimes together.

We have taught the essence of Circle – the authenticity and magnetism that happens when people allow themselves to be truly seen – to thousands of people. But, because I am a man, we do see things a *little* differently (sometimes, a lot!). I know we're not meant to talk about gender clichés, but I can only talk from my experience.

Newsflash (not newsflash), men already gather in Circle in unofficial ways. Men go on camping trips, have a beer around a campfire and tell stories. This is Circle. Me? I go and play golf with my friends. I often smile when I catch us standing in a Circle on the course talking a little more openly than we might usually do. This is Circle. I put time aside to step into nature, bond with my brothers and shrug off a bad week. This is the symbol that Circle stands for. We download over beers at the pub and, while it's not always deep conversation, we are connecting. Trust me, we are trying.

As a new dad myself, I know how easy it can be to let these times slip and not prioritise them. I know a lot of dads feel guilty for leaving their partner and child to do these activities, but they're also so important for emotional well-being.

As men, we need to demonstrate to the generations after us that talking, sharing, connecting, and using our bare hands on the earth takes us closer to home. I will personally champion that crying is good. Sharing our shitty days, and embracing our anxiety are the bravest things we can do.

So, no, I haven't described Circle in the same way that Imogen will to her people. And that's OK. Because we are learning together ... as long as we are open to learning.

Imogen, back over to you.

– Robb

The Male Calling

'There's more to men's Circle than talking about feelings. I convinced my dad to come with me. My father never hugged me and after Circle, I hugged him for the first time. My old man cried.'

– Bob

'I thought my relationship with my wife was over until I found Circle. My mate from our local gym invited me. I learnt about myself and I learnt some helpful tools that helped me talk to friends, my new Circle mates and my wife. We don't get taught this great stuff for life anymore. We need Men's Circles. I never thought I'd say this, but I needed to know about relaxation and Men's Circle gave me that.'

– Carlos

'My first reaction was, "no way", until someone told me we used to do it all the time throughout history. Once, Circle was an extremely important part of our everyday life. After going to Circle, I now know why. It's just like going to the pub with mates but without noise and booze. Great for decompression and an opportunity to download with people who will listen. In my world of office cubicles and not knowing 90 per cent of the people I work with, Circle has made my work life much more enjoyable (and productive).'

– *Anton*

'I attended a Men's Circle on the beach. We all had a swim at the end. It was great to talk and bond. It made me feel like I was part of a close-knit group. I really needed this and didn't know it.'

– *Andrew*

❍ A MOMENT FOR WISDOM

'Circle' by Peter Williams

Dear Circle,

To those who came before me, and to those who will heal after me, I see you. Growing up, I was a nervous, red-faced and lonely boy.

Fear was a feeling I felt most of the time, especially when I was around other people. I needed to be small to be safe. Using alcohol and drugs was the only way I felt better about myself; with people I thought felt better about me. I felt so alone. Loneliness has always been in my life – a complete disconnect from self.

I was never short of friends but I felt so alone in me. After being on the medical merry-go-round and anti-anxiety meds filling up my bathroom cabinet, I tried to end my life. Checking out felt like my only option. I was living in my darkest reality. But I didn't want to die. I just didn't know how to live.

It was unsurprising that I developed a crippling auto-immune disease, and my mental state was far from happy.

It was time to get help.

I heard about the Women's Circle, so I went on a search for men's groups. This is when my life changed immeasurably. After attending my first Men's Circle, I thought, 'Wow. Just wow.'

I felt nervous but not uncomfortable. I felt vulnerable but seen. I felt quiet but heard. This is where I belonged. After all these years, I found a place where I could be Peter. To share in a room with 20 men is totally different from sharing with your therapist. Peace was a foreign concept for so many years. But through this spiritual awakening, my heart finally felt at peace.

Yoga is a good example. It's likely, the majority of people in a yoga studio are women. After class, women (and the occasional man), sip tea. They talk about life with compassion and a weird sense of, 'this is all perfectly normal'. I wanted this. I NEEDED this.

I thought it was just me who had dark thoughts. I learnt that my life was not my weakness. Over time, I went from a Circle attendee to a Circle leader. Men often say to me, 'Peter, mate, you are so inspiring.' To be an inspiration doesn't always sit well with me. But now I know, to outrun depression and addiction, to stay alive when you feel capable of anything but, is inspiring. Being brave is inspiring. Surviving is inspiring when everything was heckling me to say I couldn't.

See, this is the magic. When we share a Men's Circle, we do not reject that person. We accept that man with love and respect. To express freely is liberating. The passing down of the ancient ritual of Circle is everything.

In today's world, we are missing the natural process of initiation. Not so long ago, teenage boys were sent to a forest to learn how to fend for themselves. They would come back and be seen and heard. Now, our toxic goals are suffocating our instincts. We, men, think that if we chase money, a car, a promotion, an expectation of how a man should behave, then we are a success. This couldn't be more untrue (and unhelpful). We go out and have some beers – because what else is there to do to cope? Many men are living by the values of society but not the values in their heart. And we are yearning for soul and heart connections. We are craving a 'break' from being society's version of brave.

But I can see ritual emerging. I can see the lost art of elders teaching and the young learning making a massive comeback.

As a Circle Facilitator, I lead with vulnerability. I share my baggage first. I give men the permission to not just own their truth, but to dismantle with wit. We are not robots, so why do we behave like we are?

Online is everywhere. And so is the word 'busy': 'I've had a busy afternoon, I've had a busy weekend, I've had a busy life.' Our language creates our world. Men have been lone wolves for too long and only now, are we waking up to our toxic goals. And sadly, men don't get enough quiet time. The trick is to see that success is when your inside voice is louder than the voices around you.

❍ *The masks of men*

The masks of men, a theme I often weave into Circle, are the disguises we wear: the pleaser, the joker, the sexual man, the achiever, the stoic one and the tough guy. These masks have to change and our egos have to go. Only when we learn to operate and coexist with this stuff, to fully show up, will we understand that judgement, criticism and expectation has no place in healing. Pure medicine is when men are together, mask-less and human.

Using 'I' language, also known as 'I' statements, is a way to express your thoughts and feelings in an assertive and non-aggressive way. The 'I' statements tend to make people feel less defensive and more willing to listen. This can be helpful for defusing conflicts and asserting yourself in a polite way. I urge you all to try it.

To my brothers, you may never feel ready 'enough' to step into Circle but the myth is, you never will. Just show up. How have you done life so far? You have overcome thousands of challenges, Circle is no different. The magic will unfold.

I don't just want people to feel better, I want them to actually live better, as a result. Where there are the biggest rates of male mental health decline, put a Circle in its place.

Brother, I would love to see you there. With love,
Peter

chapter twenty-two

CIRCLE FOR INCUBATING – *welcoming new beginnings*

A Circle represents the cycle of life. Circles represent a continuum, a process, infinity and wholeness. One Circle I adore holding is an Incubation Circle, a nine-month program, where the same people attend every week.

Don't be fooled by this name, this isn't about having a baby. This Incubation Circle, a concept I uniquely created is for anyone taking themselves on a journey from conception to growth and birth. This Circle is not for mothers-to-be but for those committed to a cycle of growth. And I just so happen to program the Incubation Circle for nine, lucky months.

We symbolise a nine-month pregnancy, by taking ourselves on the journey from conception to growth and birth.

At the beginning of the Incubation, I ask each Circle attendee to write a letter to themselves, that will not be opened until our last Circle. This incubation period can represent a fertility journey, a new business, new friendships and romantic relationships. It's not an overnight discovery, where you will experience your personal 'ah-ha' moment in an instant. It's about making a commitment to a future goal, hope or dream.

It's quite startling, seeing a person at the beginning and end of an Incubation Circle. I often see people who are withdrawn, sceptical even. They come to Circle prepared to change, without a clue how that will occur. Some want immediate results and it's my role, as a Women's Circle educator, to explain that nothing worth working on, changes overnight. Some have never dipped their toe in the spiritual pond, and the reluctance to fully let go is clear as day. The ego often plays a part in holding someone's progress back. But slowly, week after week, a new person is emerging. A version of themselves that has remained dormant for months, years, even a lifetime.

You might assume from the name that Incubation Circles are all about growing a baby and, in a way, there are similarities. Ironically, Incubation Circles are held over a nine-month period and they are about nurturing and welcoming in something new – but that isn't all about having a child.

I have held an Incubation Circle for various groups over the years. Women seeking an experience that spans a fixed duration tend to have a very clear intention. Some have wanted to launch a new business, others were calling in a new relationship post-divorce, and others were hoping for a baby.

An Incubation Circle is unique because it is a 'closed Circle', meaning that only those who commence the incubation period will participate until the end. We incubate together and it is an eye-opening experience. It's like the onion cliche (an oldy but a goody), because every month we strip back the layers of comfortability, complexity and resistance. There are no agendas, no KPI setting and no measurable goals.

When we incubate, we are creating.

If you are on the cusp of an adventure, going it alone doesn't need to be your only option. Freedom is everything.

Signs it's right for you:

- You're in a transition or starting a new phase of your life.
- You love nudging people to take the leap and have a 'YOLO' (you only live once) attitude to life.
- You know, from experience, that even exciting changes can come with loss and anxiety.
- Being together with a closed group of the same women, for a set timeline appeals to you.

Whether you love to see flowers bloom, wine mature or personal transformation take place, it's like teenage growing pains. It can hurt and become uncomfortable. The soul is no different. The Incubation Circle is exactly like that.

A place where birth takes place. And like any gestation period, that takes time. You cannot rush change.

The ultimate love notes

Size of group: *3–20*
Time required: *30 mins (more if bigger group)*
Resources needed: *Writing and art materials*

How the activity works: *In this activity the Circle is asked to write love letters to themselves. Playing soft music in the background can encourage loving words and safety. This letter is the ultimate self-love note. It offers an opportunity for the participants in the Circle to see themselves in a different light; to honour the goodness and moments of pride. Once the participants have completed the letter, offer them time to decorate the note with art materials, as a form of ritual and celebration. To end this activity, invite the Circle to share maybe a line or two from their personalised love letters, sharing with the group their discovery of self-compassion. As an extra act of self-love, I encourage the participants to place their love letters in a sacred place at home, as a reminder that love is always there.*

chapter twenty-three

CIRCLE FOR BABY BLESSINGWAY

As a Circle Facilitator and trainer, I have spent years gathering my knowledge to create not only Circle for women, but for specific groups of people. Planning a Circle for a group of teenagers is entirely different from how I would plan a Circle for a bride-to-be or a mother-to-be. Understanding each unique experience and what works and what doesn't, enables me to tailor and customise the experience for all those who sit in the round.

❍ *Be the baby blessed*

Women gather to empower and support one another as they step into the role of bearing and raising children. In Native American tradition (Dine Navajo to be accurate), a ceremony called a Blessingway created space for women to come together as a support Circle for the expecting mother and bless the way ahead for her. It is a web woven of the most trusted and cherished women in her life. Those who will provide a loving place where she can explore the challenges and joys that sit before her as she approaches her journey into motherhood.

As Circle Facilitators, when we hold Blessingway Circles it is our job to create an experience that focuses on making the mother feel like a queen mama. We want to cultivate activities and opening and closing blessings/meditations that honour her. This is the big difference between a Blessingway and a typical Women's Circle.

Instead of focusing on all the women in the space, we offer extra focus and attention to the mother-to-be. We celebrate and honour her journey from maiden to motherhood. It might be for her first baby or it may be for subsequent children, but this is about honouring and elevating her journey by creating a safe space for her to release and surrender any fears.

As a birth doula or birth support person, here are some important tips to anchor a mother-to-be or father-to-be:

The parents come first: A person's birth journey is one of the most important moments of their lives, so remember this as you start the journey with them.

Be the calm in the room: Mothers, fathers, and people who are about to become parents may be afraid so they will turn to you for calm, support and nurturing.

Your opinion does not matter: You are not in the room to make choices for anyone; however, you are there to reflect, support and advocate for theirs.

Be your most adaptable self: Birth is a magical rollercoaster and holding a person's hand at a moment's notice is part of your role. Your job is to adapt and serve them as best you can, no matter what curve ball is thrown at you.

'Options' is a magical word in the birth space: You are not a member of medical staff, but a provider of nurturing and supporting. You do this by providing acts like fetching water, running showers and baths, playing their chosen mood music, and offering massage, affirmations or mood lighting. You are eyes that see unconditionally, and ears that open and actively listen completely.

Keep checking in with yourself: If you are getting tired (as births can be long), take a break. Your well-being and energy levels are important too.

You don't need to be a doula to hold Circle or participate in one. I want to be super clear about that. What being a doula has taught me, is ultimately the more open and still I can be, the more I am creating a space where others will feel completely and unconditionally supported.

Being an energy creator and holder, all the roles in my life are very similar. Essentially, I am a guide or walking beside the person on their journey of learning, I encourage and nurture storytelling, both as the teller and the listener, and hold a space, gently, allowing for unfolding and discovery that is their own. My ultimate role is to honour the needs of the family; I hold a hand, I plan visits, and I sometimes make dinner for the family. Like my teachers, Renee Adair and Helen Callanan, I perform my own rituals. I remove any make-up, tie my hair in a bun and wear neutral colours. I am preparing my body (and appearance to be uncomplicated and natural). When we strip everything back, we remove room for confusion. I am the doula, the Circle Facilitator and trainer and a woman who serves the person and people who need me the most.

When the external rituals have been performed; to declutter and cleanse a space, then we go to work on our soul.

It is only then, that we can delve deeper.

I am the love in the room.

I am the non-judgement in the conversation.

I am the neutrality in the chaos.

Emotions carry so much momentum. It is always so important to provide stillness, for the emotions to move. Stillness for the grief to land. Stillness for the other person to heal. If I can be still and present and curve the bubble-up of emotions I feel, I offer a remedy that most cannot, to stare grief lovingly in the face. My stillness looks like walking barefoot in grass, or sitting by the ocean with my eyes closed. Sure, not everyone has a beach or field on their doorstep, but nature is key. Sometimes, on busy days, I sit in my shower for the few minutes I have, and let the water fall over me. In Circle and while I work I have taught myself to breathe audibly, as a kind of emotional pacemaker. People can use this as their softening tool, as they recollect and relive their grief, unstinted and unedited.

'The more you live in the present moment,
the more the fear of death disappears.'
– Eckhart Tolle

I have always loved both holding space in a Circle and having space held for me by others in Circle, but after doing my doula training, I have become more 'artful' at holding space. Holding space safely and responsibly in the modern world is key. As I have always professed, I am not a therapist, and I communicate this always very clearly. However, when someone is showing you their raw and pained self, we have a responsibility to avoid judgement, rushing the pain away, and instantly draw out a fix. Our modern world demands immediate answers where, conversely, Circle prefers to take its time. I like to mirror what a busy world cannot.

An 'artful' space holder leans into the word 'allowing'. Instead of just holding the space, you allow it to flow naturally as well. By *allowing* the space, you can keep everyone safe to communicate as their truest selves. I often imagine myself as the roots of a grand tree in this situation. Both the growth and the weather is uncontrolled by me. I allow the tree above the earth to do what it needs to while remaining steadily rooted in the ground.

Try this for yourself the next time a loved one needs you during a difficult time or situation. Be the roots of the tree, with no answers or control. Just hold the space for the tree to grow.

❍ *Baby Blessingway activity*

The activities for a Baby Blessingway should be things that are creating gifts for our mother to take with her during her labour, to have in her home in her final prenatal time or to bond the women in the Circle together. This offers the mother-to-be support during her pregnancy, birth and fourth trimester. For this reason, I like to focus on creating artworks for our mama bear, and spoiling her with a ritual such as feet bathing and the traditional cord ceremony (where we use red wool to symbolise the cord connecting mother to baby, and the invisible cord that connects us all to each other).

While the women are creating artwork for the mother, this is a good time to ask the mother to write down anything she would like to let go of and anything she would like to call in. During the Circle I would invite her to share her thoughts, fears and emotions on a piece of paper, so collectively, we can let these negative feelings go.

Here are a few examples:

Words of Wisdom through a poem or letter: In preparation for the Baby Blessingway Circle, I will email a poetry prompt to all attendees (with expectation of the mother-to-be), with a clear instruction asking everyone to create and write something special for the Queen Mama to hear on the day of our Circle. I also offer the following instructions in my email to the attendees.

Here is the poem prompt:

'Dearest Goddess Mama if I could give you anything it would be ...'

The offerings that they bring for her and the poems or letters they have created act as a creative support blanket for her during and after the time she gives birth. It's through the words shared in each poem or letter that encourages her to feel both honoured and special.

❍ A MOMENT FOR WISDOM

My first year as a mama

Parenthood is hard. There are many mothers who will share their quiet and not so quiet struggles with you. I'm tired most of the time, and I don't have the time for self-love or ritual as much as I once did. It is a sacrifice or surrendering (depending on how you frame it) and there are many things you will lose in the birthing of your child and yourself as a mother. Women are venturing from maiden to mother overnight. You do eventually gain a new version of your former self back but you do lose a lot getting there.

This is a bit of a 'taboo truth bomb' that we don't often talk about, except in safe places like mothers' Circles. And I am not talking waistlines and career fallbacks. It's more than that. It's certain freedoms and a former identity. I don't mean to be the bearer of bad news, but some things in you will die and some things you will 'birth'. There will be a lot of change to surrender to and in the wee hours of the morning when you are cuddling your tiny bundle you will know there are also many things to celebrate. This is the cycle of life. The big goal here is allowing life in and letting life go.

When you become a mother, your life becomes about another person. You are their warmth, food source, shelter, teacher and protector. That is a BIG responsibility. Even with mothers-to-be desperate to have a child, that's a big undertaking. And you don't complain if you have experienced loss, fertility challenges or even how desperate you were to have that child, for it may be interpreted as ungrateful. But it's not. It's a balancing act where rarely can you shout: I'M NOT COPING!

There are many days when I don't put on make-up or do my hair, when I live in comfy clothes and I am often covered in paint or food. This for me is so far away from many old versions of myself but there is something so natural about these moments that the more you lean into them, the more you surrender to your new reality. The more you look at the cheeky grin of your child or feel those warm pudgy hands in yours, the more you realise that life can actually be this simple, this pure and this full of love. This is what our children teach us if we allow them to.

The sheer amount of self-care I apply now is next to nothing. But I do try where I can. And you can too.

When Odette was a baby we would have baths together while I played my favourite meditation music and had salt lamps on. Sometimes she breastfed while I practised deep meditative breathing (Odette loves breathing exercises, chanting and anything that is mindful or relaxing). Times like these are rituals. No flower crowns, crystals bathing in the moonlight, but at home, do-it-yourself ritual programming. I needed to create this. Sometimes, my intuition told me to play drumming music and paint cardboard boxes after our bath. Odette plays and I let my inner child follow her.

It's never too early to incorporate your child with learning how to take care of yourself. Taking your child into the shower with you is self-love. Deep breathing close to your child is self-love. Daily reflections and affirmations into a mirror is an act of self-love. I don't have much time, but with the time I have, I choose how I absorb my daughter into the rituals and ceremonies that make me, me.

chapter twenty-four

CIRCLE FOR EXPECTANT DADS

Knowing when and how to have deeper conversations with the men in our lives is a question I get asked a lot. I wish there was a simple answer. So many of us, including myself, will analyse, strategise and formulate a plan to have those kinds of chats.

Sometimes, the dynamic can shift between two people due to a house purchase or a big move because of a career promotion, and the fears need fleshing out. These harder interactions invite men to expose their feelings and uncover their demons. This can be catapulted by the arrival of a newborn baby. When everyone's lives as they knew them pre-baby completely change.

While the energy is always different in Circle when the scales are tipped towards the masculine, the principles remain the same. It is my role as a Circle Facilitator to always ensure safety. When men have been taught that sharing is sooky, I need to perform a radical flip. Sharing is in fact, everything; sacred, purposeful and necessary.

When a mother-to-be reaches out to me, she is likely attending prenatal classes to prepare her for labour. We perform breathing exercises and visualisation techniques, but Circle is about honouring the birth rather than medically preparing for it. And for a dad-to-be, it is no different. They need to understand what their partner is experiencing on a deeper level, even though they may feel completely out of their depth with your pregnancy. It's no good wading into a one-on-one, with a list of questions (we are not interviewing our spouse).

We need to be gentle, compassionate and practical. For me, the power in Circle transcends across all people and scenarios. Witnessing the glee in a man's eyes as he prepares for fatherhood is so special, and Circle embraces fatherhood as much as motherhood, in equal measure.

And here is how.

Safety: This is key. The space Circle creates will always be blessed with no judgement, openness, and a responsibility to ensure every man in Circle feels supported.

Dig deeper into your male ancestry: We are steeped in generational bloodlines. To know the names of our grandfathers, and their grandfathers, connects a man to his wisdom. Wisdom that he doesn't know he has. It ignites an inner strength that so many don't know they even have. The answers to our inner workings are not available on Apple watches. I teach my Men's Circle Facilitators to open their Circle with an acknowledging poem, ceremony or ritual that names the men that came before them in Circle. I have witnessed men melt into flowing tears and open hearts just by saying the names of their fathers and their grandfathers. This simple act reminds each man he is not alone and never has been. Even if their father or grandfather was not present in their life they are reminded of the supporting roots of bloodlines.

Accept the shift: Homelife, work life, and pretty much life in general, is about to change with the arrival of a newborn baby. To celebrate and not fear the shift is setting a tone to surrender what is lurking beyond the labour.

Tap into the feminine: This is where the 'woo-woo' fear often appears across a man's brow. If ecstatic dance isn't your thing, that's OK. But we all have both feminine and masculine energy. This has nothing to do with biology, gender or sexuality. Masculine holds power, while the feminine hosts softness. To smoke out the inner-feminine, I invite creativity, storytelling and most importantly sensitivity.

When the baby is coming: OK, I don't want to make a sweeping generalisation, but it's not uncommon for a male partner to feel terrified and redundant during labour. By offering a man tasks and essential duties, he in turn has a purpose. Unlike the mother, the ability to bond doesn't always occur until visibility with a newborn is made. Planning ahead of time, is respecting the roles when the all-important water breaks! In Circle, we identify the roles that the man would like to take, and in turn, communicate with his partner, proudly.

See your friends as your support: It is important that we explore and identify our networks. By visualising and identifying our villages, we can prepare to trust them. Dads-to-be will need as much support as the mum. I often ask the dads in Circle, to create various scripts that would form the opening of a conversation with their friend. I ask them, 'What does asking for help sound like to you? Does asking for help feel natural, and how do you communicate a bad day?' Sometimes, we over-rehearse conversations that haven't even happened and we become embroiled in an outcome that hasn't even happened. It can sometimes be as simple as saying, 'I could really do with a talk.'

Embrace the mother: When women are pregnant, they glow. This glow is obvious and illuminating. When some men see a woman carrying their child, she is the complete embodiment of a sensual siren. Even when the unknown is firmly planted between the couple, what has been created as the product of love is sacred. Now, I am not saying that every day will be 'mother worship day' but embracing the process of pregnancy is for both of you to enjoy. This is something we talk openly about in Circle and it's great to have these deep conversations with other parents-to-be. Having multiple men in the room going through the same experiences, really helps, just like it does for women. Again, storytelling is our saviour.

Bonding with your baby: Our childhoods can be tricky. Sometimes our pasts are bordered with picket fences and family barbecues, and sometimes they are not. From broken homes to blended families, everyone has a domestic past that doesn't always fill our memory banks with excitement. But this family is your family. As a dad, you can design the family that is right for you and your partner. When the baby arrives, talk to him/her, join skin to skin and know that it all takes time.

How to prepare for the unexpected: I am going to be brutally honest. With all the love in the world, life is about to become a juggling act of sleepless nights and mess. Your needs may not always be met, and suddenly cosy date nights become six-hour stretches of nit-picking and exhaustion. It is so vital to remove expectation, move compassionately through change and know you are killing it, even on your bad days.

This can be the bumpiest and most beautiful rollercoaster there is.

Fathers-to-be

'There was something about the Circle experience that opened my heart. I felt nervous at first and didn't know what to expect, but with Imogen being such a kind person, I felt I could say anything and she didn't make me feel inadequate at all. She gave me great tools to help my wife and feel present, and so useful at our daughter's birth.'

– *Peter*

'I lost my job right before our son was born and I was so worried. Attending Circle really helped me to meet other dads and talk openly about what I was feeling. They gave me ideas and I think it helped my partner a lot that I didn't have to lean on her as much as I had been. I was able to focus on her and our baby because of going to the Fathers-to-be Circle. It's not something my father did and I didn't think I would do it, but I'll be proud to take part in my son's Fathers-to-be Circle one day. Men should be able to have more of this well-being work in their lives.'

– *Luke*

CIRCLE FOR FAMILIES AT HOME

I adore working with families. Working within a rocky family dynamic is no easy feat, but the joy I experience working with families is incredible. Most of my requests for Family Circles come from parents trying to create a harmonious home in the teenage years. So, what do we do in Circle for families? We do activities that bring us together with a purpose, like cooking together.

Do you remember the story about my first boyfriend and how his Lebanese family would show me how to cook while sharing stories? This is me giving back in abundance! Bringing people together to cook, and not just eat, is intentional creativity time. It doesn't matter if we are chopping up onions or stirring a casserole, we are tending to the family's needs.

With devices off I provide families with conversation starters that matter. This is one that you can try at home. Ask your children what they are excited about in the future? Or your wife to share a memory about the birth of your youngest? Or one that can be fun for parents (and the kids, who get to laugh) is to share something funny about yourself when you were a kid that your kids will not have heard before.

So many families are battling conflict. We are overloaded with school clubs, parties and professional deadlines but there is no time to connect as one unit. Parents offer parental guidance but have no time to bond with their children. In Family Circle, I sometimes prepare a hamper for the family and sit in the centre of the room to share snacks and nibbles. We talk and giggle. It's beautiful to see. But programming is key. I cannot show up to a house in conflict and wing my way through an urban picnic.

At times, it's hugely emotional. I have walked into families burdened with betrayal, redundancy, addiction and even death. The families are unable to shift their sadness and sometimes cooking a meal lightens the intensity that is weighing the household down.

After we share a meal, we move on to a programmed Circle with sharing and creativity. We may introduce a family game or relaxation and movement exercise. On occasions, this has turned into a dance party, which is always fun. Circle has an uncanny way of bringing the walls down, in even the toughest of hearts.

chapter twenty-six

CIRCLE FOR LOSS OF A CHILD – *finding space between miscarriage and motherhood*

My first miscarriage happened six weeks after a positive pregnancy test. I was not expecting to miscarry but then again, who ever is? In saying that, when you have experienced grief, you do start to prepare for a trauma that hasn't even happened yet. The night before my first miscarriage, I was sitting in a women's circle in my home and I remember feeling, just, WOW.

I had manifested this incredible husband, a baby on the way, and now I was creating my family. I felt complete. However, it's massively worth noting that the feeling of completeness can be met with incompleteness, and this is a cycle for all of us (where neither feeling is wrong!). The next day, I started bleeding and I was in a world of denial. For six, short weeks I was a mother. Suddenly, I wasn't. At the hospital, they assumed, because of my age, we had undergone IVF. As my bloodwork continued to change, I was losing my baby. I was becoming 'unpregnant'.

Not for the first time, I found myself craving connection and coming up against hurdles. Infertility remains so taboo, despite one in eight couples affected by this silent struggle. It really rattles me that, for something so common, we shroud it with shame.

Families tip-toe around awkward questions. Even my GP acted like it was a broken bone to be fixed, and not a broken heart. Is it because we feel like we have failed as a human? That something in us is broken? That perhaps, we are not good enough to be parents? So many people, single and in couples, quietly manoeuvre through the complexity of infertility grief, and this narrative needs to change.

Losing a child is one of the most traumatic experiences most people can imagine. Losing a pregnancy, on the other hand, is too often met with the societal equivalent of a 'shrug'. These losses, though common, are often invisible and devastatingly taboo. Many miscarriages occur early in pregnancy, before a woman has told friends or family members she's expecting. Even when loved ones know about the pregnancy, people often fail to recognise the depth of the loss. Some people, both men and women, rarely speak about miscarriage, through the stigmatised fear that they will make the person on the receiving end of this traumatic news feel uncomfortable. Others choose not to share this profound loss, as it acts as a misplaced feeling of failure.

While medical advice will guide you on how to conceive post miscarriage, rarely do we talk about the need to grieve. Grieving what 'didn't quite make it' is a social underplay that is both unhelpful and very real. Some couples may want to fix the loss quickly, adamant to fall pregnant and forget the past. Some may choose to mourn for months, even years. Living in between miscarriage and motherhood is not a one-size-fits-all remedy. Not only does a woman's body need to physically heal, a grieving process needs to take place. Some may choose to never try again, while others will try until they fall pregnant or worse, never falling pregnant in their exhausting and relentless pursuit towards parenthood.

When I was navigating miscarriage and loss, time was everything. Time, love, support and grief. I will stress this: your grief, your timeline. What works for someone else, may not work for you. Advice versus support is everything; minimal advice, abundant comfort.

Then maybe one day, the grief won't feel so foggy and dark. Motherhood may beckon you back, but it may look a little different, and that's OK. It may be laced with fear, anxiety and less hope, and that's OK too. The dreamlike state of a bump growing may be replaced with statistics rattling away in your mind. Forcing a feeling is pressure no-one needs. If you decide that you cannot walk this path, or you want to give it your all, Circle, friends, loved ones, strangers who get what you're going through, it is their love that you're going to need.

❍ A MOMENT FOR WISDOM

Losing a baby, gaining a family

One of the hardest realities a person or couple will face is the loss of a child. Whether the loss has been experienced through miscarriage or early infant loss, the devastation of creating life for it then to go, is nothing short of unbearable. For everyone who has lost someone, finding support and connection is so important. These days, we have lost many of the rituals that surround death. We have become scared to talk about or face it. After a funeral ends, the person who is grieving is expected to get on with a new version of their life. But, as a death doula, I know that ongoing support is key to learning to live alongside your grief and find hope in the future. It is the same with my work as a Circle Facilitator and creator, there needs to be more support in life's biggest moments (both birth and death) and Circles really can do that in the modern world as they have always done.

Prior to my daughter's birth, and in the early days, after my miscarriage, I leant into my Circle of wise women. They were my everything. There, I found maternal love in a different form. These women supported me, so I could support my husband. I soon became obsessed with fertility treatments, acupuncture, diet plans and anything and everything that would help us get pregnant. With a surplus of unused love, we adopted a rescue dog.

I experienced two further miscarriages and my hope was fading.

One particular day, I attended an all-day Women's Circle hosted by Shamanic healer and women's shamanic Circle Facilitator, Jane Hardwicke Collings. My wise women and storytellers did not offer me advice. They allowed me to sit in uncertainty and they knew that I had lost three pregnancies. Sitting in grief is like sitting in hell. There is no escape, no relief, and it can be relentless.

Grief, loss and trauma all come with one thing in common: uncertainty. We are so quick to appease pain, for ourselves or others, we will do anything to end the awkwardness and hardness of loss, as quickly as possible. Some drink, some overwork, some remain numb, but not sitting in uncertainty breeds exactly that, yet more uncertain times.

Pouring out our grief, can hugely benefit us, though it seldom feels like it at the time. However, you have an opportunity to reap the rewards of outsourcing your grief, and here is how:

The body keeps score: The impact of grief physically doesn't have the opportunity of denial, as it will respond to grief transparently. Those grieving may experience illness, stomach problems, nausea, trouble sleeping, muscle tightness or aches, energy depletion, headaches, and lack of appetite. These are all ways incomplete grief can manifest physically if not emotionally acknowledged.

Self-soothe your mind: Whether you are sharing or suppressing your grief, the emotional toll can be all-consuming. By sharing our grief and acknowledging our thoughts (especially the dark ones!), we can start to make sense of the loss. The impact of bottling up bereavement, can be as detrimental to our mental health, as the loss itself. By admitting to our pain, we are almost sharing and diluting the inner turmoil.

Re-energise with your people: Grief and loss, like any other emotions and experiences, can reunite people. Through grief, families reconnect, conversations are had, and communities band together, in consolidation and compassion. Through tragedy, people find comfort in coming together, and in turn, rebuilding a sense of purpose, hope and growth.

These women were not trying to fix me but allowed me to pour my fear into a space of no judgement. Without hierarchy, in its purest form, I was being held comfortably in uncomfortable pain.

The shamanic Woman's Womb Circle was exactly the healing I needed and the very next day I discovered I was pregnant with my daughter, Odette.

❍ *Preparing for birth after miscarriage*

After experiencing three miscarriages, it was hard, if not mentally exhausting, to contemplate what a real-life birth may look like. I needed my community of people so very close by, as I entered my final months of pregnancy. Without them, I wouldn't have been nearly as courageous.

My miscarriages left me questioning everything about life. I was frantic for answers and exhausted in grief. I tried to make sense of it all by attending ceremonies specifically for those who had experienced loss and grief. The doula in me knew that death is a part of life, but the Imogen in me, the pain-stricken woman in me, couldn't make sense of the pain. I would spend hours writing poetry and lighting candles as a ritual to heal. It was my own version of prayer. I would walk a lot. I would walk to this one particular park and pile up stones. There were only three in the end, the number of miscarriages that I've experienced.

While the loss was still something I was navigating each day, I did not want to give up. A tiny voice, or spark of hope you might call it, kept me moving forward. I was calling Odette, my unborn but perfectly manifested daughter-to-be, through ritual by attending a fertility Circle (held by one of my local students at the time, which was so lovely for me). I started meditating and journalling about my *called in daughter,* and what she would be like. Robb and I created an altar to symbolise our intention for her. We would talk about what parenting would look like. I'd go as far as to say that when we made love, we were consciously conceiving. In fact, I know the exact moment Odette was created.

What would life look like when she arrived?

If you have navigated your way through loss, miscarriage, rainbow babies and so much more, then you too will know the erupting emotion that comes when creating your birth plan for a baby on the way.

I knew I wanted a home birth. As a qualified doula, I have welcomed many beautiful babies into this world as the non-medical support person alongside a qualified medical team. I wanted my birth to be full of nurturing support, the kind of support that I knew would come from having a birth doula. I wanted my Circle of women around me. I also planned to invite my mother and my best friend, Sara Marie, to my home birth, to see our daughter into this world.

At 25 weeks pregnant, I was told that my baby was a 'Frank breech' baby, meaning she was lying bottom first and feet up around her shoulders and head (otherwise known as the yoga baby position). Her head was also firmly stuck under my ribs so none of the spinning baby techniques I knew were going to work. As a doula, I knew that this was always going to be a possibility and safety must come first. I had to surrender to the fact that my baby was going to be born in a hospital via emergency C-section when I went into labour.

I had my husband by my side, though my doula, who I had journalled about and imagined for years, wasn't there. Odette was born in the height of the Covid pandemic in Australia and only one support person was allowed to attend any birth. It was a subtle and quiet grief, but it was there. And the only person to remedy this grief was Odette, my daughter. The daughter who had chosen to come at this time, in this way. If you have a plan, throw your plan away. Because all the lists in the world will not guarantee the outcome. Sometimes, the outcome chooses you.

chapter twenty-seven

CIRCLE FOR THE WISE WOMAN

Though it is true that there is a wise woman in us all, in all the seasons and chapters of our lives, the wise woman who will sit with you in the Wise Woman Circle is the winter goddess. She is in her 60s or older and she is a dangerous old woman. She is not dangerous because she will harm you, she is the deepest essence of danger, she is fierce, she is fire because her fire has been burning for a full journey of life, she is also soft and full of the kind of love that has surrendered to the winter. She knows that she must keep her heart warm with the fire until spring.

Many of the wise women have raised families and have had careers or one or the other. They've lost those they love, have often faced serious medical issues, have had to learn how to get up and get on with life after numerous blows and hardships. I have seen the wise woman disregarded as being old, and shelved as someone who has lived their life. Wrong. A wise woman has felt and lived life the longest, and therefore, instead of being disregarded, she should have the loudest microphone of them all!

They have had a purpose for everyone else and perhaps now it is their time to focus solely on their inner work and their purpose of self. They may have become aware of the boundaries that have existed in their lives and they may also be very aware that they have less time now to allow those boundaries to be melted away. The wise woman seeks clarity most of all.

When you think of the wise woman, I want you to think of beauty and every shade of colour. I want you to think about endless books of knowledge and story, and to feel your way into calling all those wonderful words out to play. I want you to think of free bodies and movement and exhilaration. The Silver Queen is the woman we aspire to be. With hair so luminous that even the moon bows down to her.

I want a wise woman to think, 'The lines in my skin speak of my experiences, the silver in my hair acknowledges it. I am the crone, unconquered, untamed, with wisdom incarnated. I AM A BADASS!'

With so many Circles to celebrate, we have the opportunity to tell a story throughout the ages, warts and all. Personal storytelling is crucial to mental health recovery. A study conducted by the Cambridgeshire and Peterborough NHS Foundation Trust, UK, researched how personal story exchange can have endless health benefits. Led by Dr Kate Nurser, the findings of this study concluded that, 'Storytelling can offer a platform for experiencing meaningful connection, acceptance and validation from others, which can normalise experiences that might have previously been considered shameful.'*

❍ *Wise Woman Circle and 'writing your life' activity*

Writing can be extremely therapeutic, healing and invigorating. There is something incredibly sacred about seeing how our lives have evolved through words. The process of reflection and understanding, offers us an opportunity to bounce back in time, to the parts that shaped us, and the hardships that challenged us.

The Wise Woman Circle and 'writing your life' activity can instantly become the perfect anecdote for a 'wise woman' (and man), to untangle their pasts through the art of storytelling. So, imagine the positive impact you can have on potential Circle members' lives if you were to hold a Circle that included writing about their pasts. As a Wise Woman Circle Facilitator, you can introduce creative activities that help your attendees to map out their writing, and their own personal memoir. Creating chapter titles alone, can release emotional blockages before the life-story writing even begins.

Here are ten reasons for the Wise Woman to focus on in this activity:

---

* https://researchonline.lshtm.ac.uk/id/eprint/4650629/1/Nurser-etal-2018-personal-storytelling-in-mental-health-recovery.pdf

- Sharing personal information creates connections.
- Your family will thank you.
- You may be able to move on.
- You'll think more clearly.
- You'll feel better.
- You'll be more present.
- You'll make peace with your past.
- You'll never be bored.
- You'll leave a legacy.
- You'll have fun!

Allow the members of your Wise Woman Circle, to unleash their inner author, and celebrate their histories, with love, compassion and praise.

The most important part in understanding Circle, is that it's a notion, intention, and choice to gather, come together and heal.

A letter to courage

Size of group: *3–20*
Time required: *15–30 minutes (depending on size of group)*
Resources needed: *writing materials and music to play*

How the activity works: *Play some music and ask your Circle to drift gently into their heart space. Your Circle may choose to lie down, stand or sit, but whatever they do, they need to feel comfortable. Make closing their eyes an option. Not everyone feels comfortable doing this, so, I always say something like, 'You may close your eyes if it helps you to relax and you feel comfortable doing so.'*

Prompt with this instruction:
Please close your eyes if you feel comfortable to do so and place your hands on your heart. Relax into the safety of the room and this Circle of women. Feel into your most sacred self. Ask yourself gently: 'Dear courage, what do you want to say? Dear courage, what is it you want to say? Dear heart of my courage, what do you want to say?' Now pick up your writing materials when you are ready and please begin your letter with 'Dear Courage'. Know that what you write does not need to make complete sense, but simply allow it to flow from your heart, your intuition and your deep wise woman.

For those open to sharing their letter, encourage them with an open heart and mind, to read their letter aloud.

A MOMENT FOR WISDOM

Be authentically **not** *OK*

As a trained actor, it's no surprise that I know how to hide unhappiness or any emotion for that matter. I also know how to fake a good day. As a model, I could be deep in the middle of a rough patch and still plaster a smile on my face for the camera.

We all do it, the 'fake actor smile'. When we are going through rough patches with our spouse, and then invited to a dinner party, playing 'happy' can get us to dessert without anyone suspecting a thing. If we are unhappy in our job and the company culture is 'leave your baggage at the front door', then our 37.5-hour working week is one big, painful smile.

As we scroll through our Facebook feeds, we see good-looking people, smiling a lot. We rarely, if ever, get the whole picture behind the post. This is why safe friendships are so important. Because we all need people in our lives we can be perfectly real with. Whether that means sharing our good days or being authentically *not* OK.

I still have to work to be authentically not OK, and perhaps you do too? Trusting people with our bad days takes time, and sometimes, saying nothing is easier than spitting it out. Don't beat yourself up for not being your perfect, authentic self overnight. My first instinct is to fake being fine, even with the people who know me intimately. These are the three steps I take when I want to stop over-performing and start belonging.

Be authentic on your next bad day: When you wake up, take a personal inventory. Examine your negative feelings without rejecting or replacing them. Owning our bad days is courageous and brave. Be kind with yourself, and don't hurry to find your 'happy mask', because being authentic is being brave.

Turn off your phone, and open your eyes: I have learnt to switch off my phone, turn on my intuition and avoid the toxic rabbit hole that becomes the 'Why am I not enough' cycle. We live in a fix-it culture, where there is a quick solution for everything. When you hug next, feel how tight the grip is. Notice the next time you make someone smile. You have been, are and always will be enough.

Ask a friend the question, what do they see when they look at you? Pick a friend you trust, like, really trust. Ask them what they love about you, and what your strengths are. Ask them, 'Do you think I am a happy or sad person?' Then ask them to reverse this question. How do you see them? How others see us, is rarely how we see ourselves. We can be happy in some areas of our life, and sad in others, and that's OK too. Sometimes, we don't have all the answers we think we do. Trust.

chapter twenty-eight

WHAT I'VE LEARNT ABOUT GRIEF FROM CIRCLE

It was after hitting rock bottom in LA, that I discovered a Buddhist Centre that became my go-to sanctuary. It was my turnaround moment. It was there, I discovered one version of Circle and how it can bring people together as equals who are able to see each other just as they are and offer unconditional support. It was also at the Centre, that I learnt about the ancient principles and philosophies of Buddhism, and how this faith handles life.

There is so much synchronicity between birth and end of life. They both come as transitions and bring with them a sense of numbness, fear and, oddly, peace. Births can be painful, and death can be sacred, and the two are not mutually exclusive to one another. While life becomes the central part of any being's existence, the one thing we can guarantee in this world, is that once we are born, one day we will die. This is another theme of Circle and perhaps you can start to see and feel the power of symbolic Circles.

Both birth and death, if we approach them the Buddhist way, expose celebration, uncertainty, love and longing. Experiencing miscarriage for me was brutal and raw, and I was grief-stricken for months. When I held my daughter for the first time, I was seeing magic. I thought, how can something so precious, like motherhood, leave me both bereft, and unbelievably happy? Deep down, I felt that life had come full Circle. As we humans so often experience in this lifetime.

The topic of grief has always been a little taboo. People are afraid to talk about death because we took it away and hid it in hospitals. The parts of death we do disclose as 'socially acceptable', are when we discuss funeral arrangements, life insurances and inheritance tax.

When I speak to people in Circle, and those who I work with as an end-of-life doula, they always remember how clinical, efficient and sudden death can be. We are administratively on point (though many of us don't have our end-of-life directives in order), but emotionally terrified.

Death isn't and shouldn't be about the economy. There is no 'Project: End of life', but a series of conversations and silences that gently support the grieving process. Practical conversations are needed but filling empty silences with financial planning can mask healing.

Now I am seeing how people are becoming more 'death conscious' and listening to the wishes of those around them. For the unfortunate ones, who have witnessed life being ripped away at a moment's notice, we must hold space with what space is left.

As a doula trained to support those experiencing both birth and death, I am in complete respect and honour of those I am supporting. If you are open, they are open to you. This spills over to Circle, where I remember and teach my fellow Circle Facilitators that the most important thing you can be in anyone's journey, is to be an anchor.

'A few years ago my mum and I went to a Women's Circle together and it was the most beautiful and awakening experience. We both had an amazing time together, so we decided to attend some more. Sadly my mum passed away last year from cancer. I was very lost. My son was seven months old and I needed my mum. I didn't know what to do or where to go from there. I thought I needed to quit my job and run around; doing all these things because I knew there was something inside of me that needed to come out. It wasn't until I went to a type of "immersion" therapy with beautiful friends of mine, that I started to see the light. I had the most amazing experience and I realised that I needed to create a space for healing, to teach others how to deal with grief, including the effects of cancer.

'So I did Imogen's Honouring Heart Women's Circle program and now I have my own business page called "Come To Power".

'The story behind the name and the logo is a beautiful one. When I was very young my mother would always give me a rose quartz crystal whenever I was sad or wasn't feeling well. During her last moments in hospital, I bought her a rose quartz crystal and passed it back to her. She held it to the very end. It was like the passing of the baton, which for me is defined as "come to power". Now I am running beautiful Circles about strength and bravery, and how to deal with grief and coping with cancer. All thanks to my beautiful mother who is still very much by my side and guiding me along my way.'

– Cody

chapter twenty-nine

CIRCLE FOR END OF LIFE

As an end-of-life doula, I know how sensitive, complex and diverse death can be for a loved one. I have learnt to not fear death, or be uncomfortable among those experiencing their first, true loss. As an end-of-life Circle Facilitator, I sit with a person transitioning and their loved ones, to reduce the fear and make it a celebration.

When I meet a person who has received a life-altering and terminal prognosis, I want them to feel like they are the safest, most loved person in their world. It seems odd to me, that a eulogy is saved until the funeral and that the person's story is never recited so perfectly to them in person.

In end-of-life Circles, which are usually held sometimes days, weeks or even months, before a person is expected to pass, I ask people to share the stories with those passing, to listen to their favourite shared songs and to reminisce over photographs together. From this, I see the outpouring of love, which in essence is what I see in Wedding and Baby Blessingway Circles.

It is my role, as a Circle Facilitator, to create rituals that assist the grieving process and that honour life. When some sadly don't have the gift of planning, and a sudden death occurs, a Circle can often follow the formalities held at a funeral.

My end-of-life clients have a lot of questions. I find that the most fascinating revelation of them all. All of a sudden, there is a need to understand everything there is to know about life. They are both fading away and ignited at the same time. There is a passion in their eyes that I can't quite explain. For some, faith shifts from an unbeliever to a believer, because it brings hope and comfort. Seeing families argue over death is, sadly, very rife. The person passing away may have very different versions of what they want from their next of kin. Turbulence often outweighs compassion. But anger and grief tend to exist side-by-side. My goal in Circle, is to defuse this anger and provide ways to soften the fear of bereavement, and provide a soft landing for everyone when the grief takes hold.

If you are navigating your role with a person you love in transition, be an anchor in the room. Offer love, light and celebration if you can. Sometimes, I simply offer cups of tea and actively listen. There is no wrong way to grieve.

As an end-of-life doula there are so many similarities with welcoming new life. In fact, the synchronicity of birth and death is incredible but that is a whole other story. Here are some tips to anchor a family as they commence one of the most difficult stages in life.

This isn't about you: Leave all your baggage at the door. In other words, be neutral and open to anything. No end-of-life journey is the same and the only person's vision that matters right now is the person who is on the journey. Your job is to walk beside them, not lead the way. Which may feel strange at first.

Imagine your heart is a third ear: Listen through it as deeply as you listen with your ears. This will help ground you in each moment with every word that is spoken in the space. By space I mean the home, the hospital or hospice, or the cafe where you are meeting your client and/or their family.

There are going to be big feelings: Often, at the end of life there are big emotions like fear, anger, grief, panic, anxiety, depression and stress. I've seen these many emotions play out in Circle too. As a doula, it is your job to allow all these emotions, not only for the person passing, but for all their family and friends. This doesn't mean you burn yourself out holding space for the overwhelm, but be conscious of all stages of grief. Which brings me to the next, very important, point, boundaries!

Boundaries are extremely important: You may not always say these aloud, but it is important to define your own limits. For example, your time. End-of-life journeys can be long and hard, but they can also be joyful and short. For the longer journeys, it is extremely important that you don't burn yourself out. If you do, you will not be able to serve the person you are supporting at your best.

Provide the best care: This important point was passed on to me by my end-of-life mentor, Helen Callanan, who created the end-of-life Doula training, Preparing the Way. Every single person you serve deserves the best possible care. What this means, is understanding what care you can provide. There may be something a person asks for or needs, where you are not the person to provide it. This is an important part of being a doula, being able to refer, delegate and discover services, people, products or places, that can best fulfil the needs of the person passing. Remember that magical word, 'options'!

chapter thirty

GRIEF DOESN'T WANT TO HARM YOU

I often wonder if grief offers comfort. Grief acts as a bridge, between the loss and the letting go. It's as though grief is a person. The first person you meet after you say goodbye. The first person to see your last kiss. The person who is there from day one. Before we know it, grief is an ally, and saying goodbye to grief, is saying goodbye to the only other witness to those last mortal moments.

The modern-day world is a lot deeper than we give it credit for. We are more magical and colourful in the way we process pain. Help and support is more accessible than ever, however, there is a dark side too. An unspoken side in a middle ground, that while services are on the rise, the stigma surrounding asking for help remains very common..

We are so informed; sometimes too informed. The internet is not short of blogs, articles and journals on the infamous five stages of grief. Some of us, who are goal driven, approach grief the same way as we approach work, hitting each stage, ticking it off and comparing our results to someone else's. For some people who are governed by the stages of grieving, they judge themselves too. They judge themselves for not completing a stage soon enough or efficiently enough. So, they label themselves a 'failure at grief'. Our friends might say, 'I don't think you have processed your anger yet', as though grieving is a textbook procedure. Let me reassure you it is not. I recently read a quote on a friend's Instagram post whose grandmother had said about grief, 'It is just more love than I know what to do with,' so let this thought wash over you and allow it into your heart for a moment. For me this feels like one of the wisest takes on grief I have ever heard.

Breathe.

When our pulse is racing, and our breath shortens, this is a sucker punch reminder from your body, asking you to consciously breathe. To focus on the inhale, and release on the exhale. It sounds simple, but it's not always that way. So breathe some more. Breath is never something to be afraid of, in all of life's ups and downs, breath is always your best friend.

A Buddhist friend once told me that remembering to consciously breathe at least once a day is as important as eating, drinking and sleeping. I try to consciously breathe when I get in the shower, before a meal and when I lie down to sleep. Three simple deep breaths that fill your lungs with oxygen completely will recharge you, relax you and immediately reconnect you to your body. Most of us constantly have shallow breaths and you will really notice the comparison when you practise conscious breathing.

❍ *Get to know your grief*

Getting to grips with your grief and knowing its role in your life can make the process softer. When we understand an emotion, we can learn its role and power. When we identify grief and get up close and personal with the pain it inflicts, somehow, it becomes less of a stranger to us.

Timelines don't work: Give yourself the time to mourn. Over time, the grip that grief has on us will start to weaken, soften and eventually grief will stop narrating your choices. But avoid setting goals that include time, such as, 'By March, I will be healed.' Losing a loved one is hard enough. Don't add extra pressures, after all, healing is never linear.

It's OK not to cry: We go into a state of numbness when we lose a person we love. Being in a trance-like state is nature's way of protecting us from tragedy. Crying is not a benchmark nor is it on any set of criteria. Crying works for some, but it's not the same for everyone. Grief is a state of shock. Our emotions are frozen. When ice thaws, the water comes. Tears can be a little like that.

I lost my second grandmother while writing this book. I haven't cried yet. I can't explain it and I don't know if or when the tears will come. My mother has found this extremely difficult, as she has cried a lot. I was also unable to talk about this passing in our family. Again, I have no explanation for this grief experience. I haven't grieved like this before but I have learnt enough by sitting in Women's Circle, that we must always try to allow that which we can't explain. Even when it is hard for those around us (who might expect a different reaction from us), we must honour our individual experience and let things be as they are. It is always OK not to cry. There is a freedom in knowing this.

Grief causes depression: I know this is stating the obvious. But when we are grieving, we are also dealing with the secondary symptoms of depression, a double whammy of an emotional blow. Please go easy on yourself. The body doesn't know what has happened on the outside, just what is happening on the inside. It will react to stress responses, anxiety and overwhelm. In the early days of grief, apply the same tools to grieving that would be applied with depression: eat, walk, talk and be kind with every milestone, even if it's taking a shower.

Guilt and grief: Guilt is an unhelpful emotion, no more so than when it creeps in during the throes of grief. We grieve what we did say or didn't. The pain we may have caused or the love that we didn't express. We may feel guilt under the circumstances of the loss. It is so important to understand that regret plays a huge role with grief. But let go of the guilt, please.

Grieving is normal: I would like to preface this by saying, there really isn't any such thing as normal. When panic steps in, so does a franticness in trying to re-establish the life we had, before overcoming the loss of a loved one. There is no normal way to grieve. Your version of normal is unique to you. Confusion, chaos, and conflicting feelings are typical, but never normal. Comparison is a word that we should try to surrender to. Surrendering to the 'gatekeeper', a term often used by therapists which outlines the process through which ideas and information are filtered, speaks volumes here. There is no comparison in grief and this is something that we individually and as a culture need desperately to let go of. Your feelings are valid, and feelings will not harm you. Your normal will return, or a new normal will emerge!

One day, it will feel different: Coexisting with loss and hope will replace the desperation and confusion felt in the early days of grief. If we smile at a joke, or enjoy a day out with our friends, our memories remain sacred. You will start to make plans and feel ambitious again.

Learning to love life again is not an insult to grief.

Like motherhood, we do not have all the answers. But like my role as a mother, to farewell life, is to nurture and not know it all.

chapter thirty-one

CORPORATE CIRCLES – *making it work at work*

We've already touched on some Circles in this book – Mothers Circles, Fertility Circles, Wedding Circles. But, what about Circle in a corporate setting?

In recent years, we have seen a 'mindfulness spike', with businesses budgeting in well-being practices. I know it can be intimidating to receive an email invitation to join a 'Wellness Circle' in your workplace, but I've also seen it have an amazing impact on office morale.

It's all about finding the sweet spot where people can venture outside their comfort zone but also feel safe to share, be vulnerable and present.

It takes a carefully designed and well-thought-out program to ensure that everyone is exposed to Circle but not forced into it, especially in the workplace. When I'm facilitating a Corporate Circle, my role is to find the words that will elevate the experience in the room, and not overwhelm the attendees.

Instead of using phrases such as 'meditation', I use 'relaxation'. Instead of stoking the spiritual flame, I talk about the Buddhist philosophy, 'life conditioning', without mentioning that it is Buddhist philosophy. We know that words carry weight, and it's these simple exchanges that encourage relatability and not a feeling of fear.

So, don't worry, if you cross Circle paths with me in a corporate training room, I won't lay out my tea light candles and incense. My biggest goal as a trainer is to help you learn that we need to be the head of our group, to guide and never to lead.

Letters from Corporate Circle

'I run an online fashion business with 28 women who are based in multiple countries. Support and connection is really important to our team, yet not easy to achieve when we all work remotely. I met Imogen at an event and she encouraged me to facilitate an online Circle on a regular basis, to bring my team together. At first I didn't think this would be anything different from other well-being workshops and activities, but with Circle,

something truly wonderful happened. We no longer felt like a separated team and me, a leader with hierarchy; we felt supported together. As a CEO, I believe it is the deep connection that the process of Circle provides. We began to see each other as deep, thriving and complex beings. I started seeing genuine support offered and that was reflected in our team's ability to achieve. Circle is an incredible gift. It is simple in its approach and yet powerful beyond words.'

– *Elaine*

'My workplace felt like it was missing something. We all knew each other as colleagues but not as people. Circle gave us all a safe space to come to and relax. It became a place where all competition and work stress was left at the door. I really enjoyed the creative activities and I believe we all felt like circle helped us with our stress at work and at home. It became my favourite day of the month.'

– *Angela*

'Imogen came to our work and introduced us to Circle. We are a small team so we all participated, both men and women. I work in the fitness industry and there is a lot of support and avenues for health and fitness, but not always mental health and well-being. I felt like Circle addressed well-being in new ways and we were all able to get to know each other better.

We could speak freely and really enjoyed the activities. It felt like "part party" and "part soul-searching" talk time. It was very recharging. We all love it and still do Circle every two weeks on Friday mornings.'

– *Sam*

chapter thirty-two

FRIENDSHIPS CAN SAVE US

If a relationship ends, a loved one passes, or a devastating blow has hit a family dynamic, our friendships are often on speed dial. In a way, we can be closer to our friends than our own family members, because oddly (or not!), we get to choose our best friends but not our bloodlines.

So, you've read my story and learnt a little bit (well, a lot) about me. You've heard how I arrived at Circle through the break-ups, breakdowns and breakthroughs. How I wandered the streets of LA with a broken heart and found myself stumbling into my first Circle, which saved me.

As a teenager, I was obsessed with religion, and mythical stories. I didn't want to live under any one particular faith but I yearned to learn. I remember being referred to as a wise thinker at school, and at the time it wasn't a compliment. I was inspired to understand what makes us tick as humans.

The power of Circle is about connecting with other people, but first, we really need to know ourselves better. What is stopping you from making genuine connections: Do you believe you're not enough, that you're *too* much, that you're not deserving?

The big question is: How do we know when we've hit the red flag that surviving alone isn't working for us?

Let me tell you – when you know, you know.

Throughout my life, I have been blessed and lucky enough to have met so many incredible women. Some were with me through my difficult seasons and some are now my best friends, teachers, mentors and confidantes. I couldn't have gone through any of this without them.

We all know that feeling when we just need to talk to a person who 'gets us'. A person we can tell our secrets to, both good and bad. Who handles our grief without fear or hesitation. A person who doesn't judge us but instead rallies from the sidelines, who loves us unconditionally and isn't afraid to say when our choices may not have been the kindest on ourselves. Friends like this are hard to come by. We must hold on to them, even when there are oceans, families, commitments and jobs in the way. Nowadays, it's not uncommon for our loved ones to be scattered across countries. With our new luxury of digital accessibility, a Facetime call, or Zoom hang-out can be made at the click of a button. Sometimes, it's also so lovely to send a note or a card. Something that has been touched by you, and mirrored in the way your handwriting curls. Sure, it can all take a bit more effort than a drive down the highway, but connections and love require effort, and … a little more effort from time to time.

I believe that there are different types of friendships. That comes from experience and knowing that, sadly, friendships can fade; that their purpose was to exist but not be ours forever (and that's OK too). We need friendships but sometimes, the stoic among us, pretend we don't.

Friendships for a little while: Sometimes, we form friendships to fulfil a purpose. Perhaps you are taking up running and feel motivated by having a run-buddy next to you. You may be forming a passion project where someone feels inspired to do the same, and your friendship is the backbone to its success. This type of friendship is made by a shared purpose, structure and familiarity. Confessionals don't take place, but a bond and respect is nurtured to achieve a goal. They might just last a year but they are not your forever friend and that's OK.

Friendships for a chunk of time: You may have moved to a new neighbourhood or company, and you have formed a friendship based on your circumstances. There isn't just one likeness but you have crossed paths rather than sought out a person to divulge every bad day to. Conversations revolve around the same topics and rarely do you enter into each other's private lives, but you know where they live. This friendship is based on trust and continuity but if circumstances were to change, such as motherhood or relocation, they may not withstand too much change. You will always message on birthdays and over the holidays, but there is no expectation on either part to synchronise diaries for calls, catch-ups and visits.

Friendships for a lifetime: The most perfect friend in your life, who you don't need to talk to for months on end for your bond to be unbreakable. This friendship can handle big change. In fact, this friendship encourages happiness for both of you, despite the consequences it may have on your time together in-person. This person knows your darkest days, biggest wins and nothing is off limits when you talk. A lifetime friendship is one of your big loves. You would move mountains for them if they needed you to and your souls over time have intertwined. This type of friendship should be held like gold for it's invaluable, irreplaceable and knows no bounds.

One important thing I've learnt is that a friend-affair is no different from a romantic relationship, minus sexual attraction and physical intimacy. I have embraced my friends, held them and fought for them. We must not lose sight that friendships are necessary in order for us to feel supported and less alone.

We can argue with friends, break up and make up with them. We must have the 'conversation' when it comes to boundaries or if something isn't right. If friendships hold a place in our heart that is as sacred as our partners, or family members, why should a friendship have less attention or work? It's a weird scenario, navigating through a bumpy patch with a bestie, but nothing beats a conversation that is based on honesty, and when you can absolutely say, 'I love you, I want you in my world and I miss you.'

activity: say it with love

Collective love poem

Size of group: *4–20*
Time required: *15 mins*
Resources needed: *writing materials*

How the activity works: *This is the ultimate, collective love poem. The Circle will begin by holding hands and chanting together the word 'love'. Think of words, breathing and hand-holding as a collective rising up of women, a rising up of sisterhood and this Circle. This activity is a pure rising up of our love for all those sitting in Circle, and this poem is an outpouring of the pure love that we are able to conjure collectively. Together, chanting the word 'love' for five minutes raises the energy within the Circle space.*

Begin by saying the word 'love', and those in the Circle will slowly join the chant. You can sing it, or chant it like you have heard yogis do with the sound of 'Om' in a repetitive and unified rhythm. I like to start soft and get louder and more joyful but that is my choice, you do not have to do the same. After a few minutes, it starts getting softer and slower so people know that the chant is coming to an end and then, ring a bell to seal the chant. Now the Circle will write poems together. Before long, you will feel the beautiful vibration of love. One person will write a statement on a piece of paper about love to get the activity started, before passing it to the person on their left, and so on. There is no need to rhyme or for the poem to make perfect sense, but trust that it will once finished. Once finished, you can share the collective poem, so everyone can write it down, as the perfect Circle keepsake.

Note: If you choose to do this activity alone, opting for a seven-day period of poetry writing can unlock so much spontaneity and the perfect outpouring of love. This is also a beautiful activity to do with your family – if you are all game.

chapter thirty-three

YOU GOTTA LOVE A GOOD CLICHÉ

The age-old cliché of 'loving yourself' can be annoying when single, but clichés become a go-to Google search for good reason, because they are often true! Until we truly understand how to love, we cannot love. Until we see ourselves as worth loving, people won't love us. If we don't know how to understand love, we won't know how to ask for it. You wouldn't go to watch a movie in French without subtitles if you couldn't speak French. So, you cannot have a loving relationship, if love hasn't been felt.

Sometimes, we manifest repetition in relationships. It's the very baggage we carry. We often ask ourselves, 'Why am I so unlucky in love?', despite not really changing much about our part of the process. I would often go into relationships with the assumption that all men were unfaithful and not to be trusted. I put my hands up to this incorrect, massive generalisation. I don't know if we are always unlucky in love but strategically hard on ourselves when it comes to making better choices.

'Comparison is the thief of joy.'
– Theodore Roosevelt

Expectations can taint our support systems. Forming a support system is like forging an emotional army. We have to pick the best people to have in our camp; the kindest, the most loyal and those who will always have our back, no matter what. To find Robb, or for Robb to find me, I needed to break down the programming in my heart as to what I was looking for. And that took work. It took me owning up to the part I played in my past.

I want you to ask yourself these questions, to further uncover and discover how you seek out the support of your someone special.

Are my boundaries in place, and have I shared them? This is a biggy for sure! As I shared in a previous chapter, boundaries are for everyone's emotional safety. They are not there to act as a fortress but a 'kind-ness' contract to honour our needs, values and hopes for a happy and healthy relationship.

Is this relationship serving me or keeping me company? I am a big believer that sometimes we fall in love with the idea of falling in love rather than it being the real thing. Why? Because we get lonely. There is nothing more exciting than seeing your phone light up late at night or the sound of a key turning in the door after a day of being bored and alone. Relationships are not hobbies. People are not activities. Knowing the difference is a hard but simple truth.

Am I being honest with my needs? Your needs are not just if you like a dash of milk in your coffee each morning or that the kids need picking up when you are running late. Your needs could be for more touch, affection, alone time, company, deeper conversations, or silence. Do you know your needs and can you ask for them to be met? It's hard to remain resentful when someone is trying so lovingly to meet the needs that we articulated. **Am I being kind with their needs?** If you are feeling lonely, chances are they are too. If you are feeling like sex has sloped off into the abyss, chances are, they do too. Have they got a work promotion you aren't that interested in or have you road blocked a trip away? Exchanging needs is a two-way street.

Do I feel emotionally safe? This is a massive deal breaker for me, in all relationships. For so long, safety around relationships, quite rightly, has focused on the physical. We are encouraged to know our physical limits, exit strategies and options should we physically feel that we're in harm's way. But how about emotionally safe? When we enter into a supportive union with a partner, we need to know if they can absorb our vulnerability. It is so important to know that you will be heard, understood and cared for in the parts of your life that will be unplanned and difficult. When times do get tough, will they find a place of stillness, until the sun shines again?

'I had a calling to facilitate Women's Circles because I wanted to create a safe space to be of service to other women. It is a place of love, safety and support. Circle is about honouring what it means to be female with strength, support and wisdom. A sacred space for women to connect with each other; to their heart space and mind. A place to heal and learn from each other, while nourishing the soul. A time to honour your uniqueness and your voice. A place where we can speak from our hearts, free of judgement. A place where we can embrace each other just as we are, in all our messiness and beauty.

Circle is a sacred gift to feel seen, heard and connected. A time to be kind and compassionate to ourselves and a space to share our truths. Circle is a non-judgemental, caring, informative and confidential space. Circle is a soulful immersion for women; an opportunity to give and receive, replenishing and refreshing our emotions. A PLACE TO FEEL INSPIRED!'

– Jacinta

chapter thirty-four

RADICALISE YOUR FRIENDSHIPS

One of the powerful benefits of participating in women's groups and being a Circle devotee and creator, is knowing how to hold space for lifelong friendships, whether we see each other in person or not. We can go months, even years without speaking, but when we do, it's like nothing has ever changed. If you are longing for belonging, and true connection, the steps and stages to discovery are easier than you think.

Here is my fast-track version to true connection, where being 'heart smart' can be found in five, doable steps:

Step One: Is it just me feeling this way? Is there someone you feel an instant connection and familiarity with? Does their persona intrigue you and you have this urge for them to be your friend, but you don't know why? Perhaps, you are craving a friendship where you can speak your truth and you will be heard. Reach out to this person and nurture this instinct. When you speak to them, observe their body language. Are they paying attention to what you are saying with engaging eye contact, concentration and steadiness? Are they jumping straight into advice giving or are they actively listening? The more we listen and learn, the more the person will mirror our behaviours. Providing a safe space, where you can say exactly what you need to, is a friendship worth exploring.

Step Two: Can we be friends? You have formed a connection and feel the frequency of interactions are increasing. This may not always be feasible but for now, it's perfect. You get the same buzz when you receive a text message from them, much like with someone you have just started dating. The friendship is exciting and you feel lighter knowing they are in your life. Foster the connection. Commit to purposeful and intentional time. Slow down the pace at which you speak and your breathing. Even lessen the movement. If you are standing near your kitchen bench, perhaps sit down and see if they follow. If your movements and mannerisms are starting to mirror each other's, layers of comfortability are growing.

Step Three: Having the 'What are we?' chat: I know, it sounds weird. In romantic situations, most have the need to define the relationship: are we dating, exclusive and is there a future in this? Why should this be any different for friendships? Sure, romantic relationships can offer us so much but friendships can rescue, save and restore us. Vocalise your expectations with your friend. Don't be afraid to share the moments you felt fearful, neglected or jealous even. If they are pregnant, and you are in your darkest IVF days, let them know that you are struggling with dual feelings. Maybe you lost your job, and your best pal just hit a six-figure salary, or you just found out you have to move out of your rental and they just bought their first house. Perhaps you just broke up with your partner, and your friend just got engaged? Openness can prevent confusion and conflict. We need boundaries with people for familiarity and unfamiliarity. Boundaries are healthy practices for you and for those around you. Be a boundary-setter and see how your inner stories shift from unanswered questions to self-assurance and certainty.

Step Four: Boundary-setter's assessment: This step doesn't have to be a big and awkward moment. Friendships are also about frivolity and not just intense moments. But, it is also very important to offer a proviso before the harder conversations.

Settle into a script a little like this: *Before I share something deeply personal with you, please may I say that I don't want advice. I really just want to share. Are you able to hold space for me? Are you able to have this conversation just to listen? If you ever need this, I am capable of holding space for you too.* (Wait for a moment. Read body language. Pause. Check in with your boundaries.) The more you say it, the more natural and second nature it will feel.

This goes against everything we naturally feel as humans – we need to fix, advise and resolve. But it's not our only way. Remember what I said about problem comparisons? We mean well, but we block the space for healing to occur if we rush into quickly solving it.

Step Five: Take your time seriously: A friendship is a deep relationship based on love and it has to be the right kind of love. We accept behaviour in friendships that we wouldn't with our partners. But I suggest we should try to understand why there is a possible difference. We don't invest in the same way with our friendships as we do in our romantic relationships determining, what's working and what's not working. We've stopped talking about our needs with other women. That is why we need time. Friend-affair time. Not just a coffee date, or a yoga class together, but carved out, uninterrupted time.

Circle has created friendships for me. I didn't always find meeting new friends or nurturing friendships easy. Spending quality and intentional time with women in a Circle, has not only given me the confidence to spark new friendships, but it has really helped me to see that I am a great friend. I have a lot to offer and the women in my Circle have reflected this to me.

Chat your way to inner peace

Size of group: *3–20*
Time required: *20–40 mins*
Resources needed: *writing and journalling materials*

How the activity works: *Lead with a journalling prompt to inspire this activity. Ask participants to take out their journals and begin by writing, 'I am welcoming a conversation with my inner peace, I am inviting my most peaceful self to speak with me at this moment.' Then freely write whatever comes to mind. It can also be helpful to play some music for ten minutes so as to let the creative juices flow. Allow ten minutes for free writing and then encourage your writers back into the Circle space. Perhaps, ask the Circle if anyone is willing to share. You might also choose to have some prepared questions about peace to start a conversation such as, 'What is your definition of peace?', 'What inspires peace in your life?', and 'What do you think is missing from your life in order for you to feel more peaceful?' Then, let the inner peace settle.*

❍ A MOMENT FOR WISDOM

When you find your edge, you find your magic

I remember my first Kundalini yoga class (a type of yoga that involves chanting, singing, breathing exercises, and repetitive poses). It was intense but brilliant! There is a lot of groaning, moaning, and it is not for the faint-hearted, but it is for the spiritually curious. It scared the pants off me to start with.

My eyes were closed, and I could hear the weird sounds circling around me. I had no idea what was going on, but I liked it. I was finding the woman in me who didn't want to conform anymore. I was discovering the person who didn't want to look a certain way, date a certain guy and live a certain life.

Since that moment, I've always tried to hold space for those people who come to Circle even though they're not quite ready and don't feel comfortable. For me, this is where the magic tends to happen – when you're moving into an area and an emotion you haven't experienced before.

In one particular Circle, a friend of mine brought another friend along. She was a police officer and when she arrived, she was still wearing her uniform. She confessed to me that she was 'straight-laced and sceptical of whatever Circle was, but her friend had convinced her to come'. I loved that level of honesty because she wasn't telling me what I wanted to hear but that she was open to trying. As friends, they were total opposites.

When she left, still looking formal and law-abiding in her uniform, she turned to me and said, 'I cannot guarantee I will be back. This is possibly not for me. But there was something I loved, and I don't know what it is yet. But there is something.' That was a massive moment for me because although her eyes were open in meditation, scanning the room for clues as to 'What's coming up next?', her soul and heart were game.

I've talked a lot in this book about comfort zones – the places where the magic happens. Like falling in love, any new experience can be scary, terrifying, unnerving … and brilliant.

When I feel wild and free, slightly uncomfortable even, I know I'm moving into something I haven't discovered about myself before.

Stepping outside your comfort zone can be exactly where you need to go.

chapter thirty-five

LEARNING TO TRUST

I have not always felt safe around women. I don't mean physically safe, but emotionally. As though somehow, I was never good enough to be one of them, or be accepted by them. Perhaps you feel the same way? This isn't by any means a fault or negative observation, but a realisation that being on the outside of a Circle, is a perfect calling to being in one. For a long time, working in a competitive culture took the potential from what could have been beautiful connections. I compared myself to women. Sometimes, I envied them. I worried that, if they succeeded, I wouldn't. I was scared to really be myself in their presence.

Today, I feel entirely different. I want all women to be successful, however they choose to define success. I want this book to empower, inspire and motivate people to become the best versions of themselves. But more important than that, I want you to be YOU.

My hope is that we live our truth and do so unapologetically. For some of us, we have spent months, years and even decades shrinking ourselves to fit in. We have worn masks and facades to abandon who we are and, in turn, our truth because we fear that perhaps, the 'real us', won't be accepted. And if you find this a little too overwhelming, I give you permission to lie down, absorb and rest. I for one, have your back, you are safe!

Today, I see the women in my life as my soul family. Knowing how to select your inner circle is a gift, not a given. We all have felt like our very own 'Miss Independent' at one point or another. But, think about a time you felt the strongest, softest and most resilient in your life. Were you alone or was there at least one woman pushing you forward? It's not a coincidence that, when we gather as women, we are able to achieve incredible things.

Unfortunately, for some women, we are held back by a fear of female friendships – whether we will be welcomed, whether we are worthy and whether we can all succeed together. I'm here to tell you: you ARE welcome, you are worthy, and we are more likely to succeed when we support each other.

So, take the first steps to female friendship freedom. The first and ultimate step is trust that you do belong. That your story, beauty and uniqueness can offer so much, and that in turn, your friendships need you, as much as you need them. When you ultimately trust that there is a different way to form a friendship; when comparison making is flung out the door, yumminess in the collective of others like you, is there for the taking.

❍ *Debunking myths about female friendship*

Groups of women are so mean: Yes, this can be true, but mixed groups of men and women can also be catty if you choose the wrong group of people. You are in control of curating your friendship group and looking for people with good vibes only. If you have had bad experiences with women in groups, Circle may feel like yet another group of women to avoid. This couldn't be further from the truth. When I leant into my very first Circle, I felt immediately accepted. There was no dress code, career stories or success criteria. There were no demands on me to be 'Circle ready'. Now, groups of women have become my most sacred asset.

She's already got so many friends – why would she need me? As we move through life, there is always an opening for new friendships because our circumstances constantly change. As a fairly new mother, I still value my single friends, but I also crave friendships with mothers who get my challenges. This is true for everyone in every stage of life. So, here we go with numbers again. We measure so much by the number of social media followers we have, friends in our camp, and dollars in the bank. However, when a friend enters your life, remember, you are not imposing on this relationship. They chose you too.

If I do it alone, I'll somehow be rewarded. Ugh: We can wear our ability to 'endure' as a badge of honour. But, being resilient can also be exhausting and debilitating. Imagine if we could see leaning on people as a strength instead of a sign of weakness. I like to think that most of my biggest wins have been orchestrated by the good choices I made, alone. When I met my husband, Robb, I wasn't looking for a big, movie-like ending. I was so happy in myself, that anything on top was a bonus. I knew I could do life well solo, but I no longer wanted to. When we get to knowour needs from our wants, going it alone can also be massively unnatural to our innate human make-up.

I should be happy alone: Yes, we all need to love ourselves. But it's pretty awesome to be loved by someone else too. Happy people also need friends, just as much as people who are struggling. In good times and bad, I crave positive interactions, moments of rest and opportunities to recharge. Can I just say, I am not a fan of the word: should. When we 'should' do something, it's almost like giving or receiving an order. Yes, roam freely, and make the magic happen because it's what *you* deserve. I am ridiculously happy with the family and home that I have created. Writing this book is me being happy alone, because I knew that one day, I needed to share Circle with the world. But, I adore the fact that I can share my alone wins with my family. And there is nothing 'should' about that.

❍ *Who is the modern woman?*

She is complex, she is busy and she wears many hats. There has been a huge surge in the wellness industry in recent years, yet the modern woman often puts herself at the bottom of the pile. The boom to live a more mindful existence is because we are trying to learn an ancient ritual that has been lost over time: to trust and connect.

Yet the modern-day woman may still be clutching a green juice, alone. She is insanely busy and exhausted. A modern-day woman wants it all but has no time to enjoy her own successes. Her comparison making is holding her back. In my early career as a model and actress, I lost count of how much time I spent wondering if I 'measured up'. Not just physically (though that was a massive part too!), but emotionally, intellectually, and did I have what it takes to live in the entertainment world? Everyone around me would say, 'yes'. However, inside, I was buckling under the pressure of constant comparison. While I loved my work, I hated the constant questioning, which was holding me back from even more success.

What this modern woman needed was Circle; a safe place to recharge, reconnect and to remember just how powerful a group with the intention to support and accept without question could be.

❍ *Why we feel the need to be strong (alone)*

Whether you are discovering or reclaiming your power, your fierceness is contagious. Nothing turns heads faster than a woman who knows her worth. But, somewhere between Hollywood blockbuster movies and the inspirational speaker circuit, women have been encouraged to 'go it alone'. We can do it all, have it all and we don't need to rely on anybody ... or do we?

Who is this Miss Independent?

Is it the woman who is perpetually busy? The mother-of-three who can breastfeed while her Zoom camera is off during a work call? Or the woman who claims that relationships aren't for her, while she puts the key in the door with no-one on the other side to welcome her home.

I'm not saying that every independent woman is miserable. But, I do think a lot of us are exhausted from over-coping; from doing it all, from being it all and never feeling safe to lean on anyone.

Don't get me wrong. I am the first to cheer if I see one of my friends or clients uncover their 'completeness'. But I also want people to realise it isn't the only option. You can be a strong, independent woman and still be in a loving and supportive relationship. You can move across the world and still talk to your mum every day. You can lead a team of 50 and still want someone to make decisions for you sometimes.

It's time we gave ourselves permission to be stronger together, not alone.

❍ *Friendships through the ages*

The most important female friendships in your life might not look like the cast of *Sex and the City*. The best female friendships transcend all backgrounds and ages. In fact, we have so much to learn from people who don't fall into our specific 'category'.

Now, I search for the 'wise woman', who has lived, learnt, and let go of what does not serve them. I absolutely cherish, as a Wise Woman Circle Facilitator, all that she represents. The wise woman, the dangerous old woman, the midwife and the splendid hag. The wise woman is everywhere, truly, and while this sounds like a huge generalisation, she is your neighbour and the woman strolling to the shops each morning. She is the woman sitting alone on the park bench, desperate to tell you her stories. She is the mother of all mothers and the grandmother of all grandmothers. She has lived a life and is full of knowledge and great secrets. She looks frail on the outside, but inside, she has a resilience that comes with a life lived. Ultimately, self-confidence, feelings of trust and celebration in the great woman she has grown into.

'Early on in life, I realised I was different from others. When I was in a car accident at five years old, my face no longer looked the same as it once did. I was left with a massive scar, which may have scared some. My direction changed from then on, as I knew how it felt to be left out and wouldn't wish that feeling on anyone.

'I spent my childhood and teenage years making sure everyone was welcomed, loved and included. It was then that I formed some beautiful friendships along the way. As I got older, with my family slowly moving away from my hometown, I began searching for something else. I took a healing journey and by doing so, I longed for deeper connections. I wanted to find my soul family. I am an introvert by nature, and I feel comfortable bringing others into my space, in Circle. I work with many clients from my home-based studio, being a holistic practitioner in the energy-healing field. I realised that a lot of souls wanted to find new friendships, with others searching for the same.

'I saw Imogen's post on social media about Circle Facilitator training, and I knew it was a sign. But, I didn't know where to start or how to go about it. I just knew I wanted to help bring back a sense of community and connection.

'It was a relatively easy decision, deciding to invest in Imogen's Circle Facilitator course. I felt supported and

learnt more than I could have ever imagined. She has a beautiful light and warmth. I could feel her embrace us, as she shared her knowledge and teachings. I completed the course three years ago. I have held many different Circles since. It is an absolute honour and privilege to do this work, and I absolutely love holding space for all who attend my gatherings. The world certainly needs more of us to shine our light in our communities, and I am so grateful I took the steps I did. I have found my village which continues to only keep growing.'

– *Rebecca*

chapter thirty-six

MOVING THROUGH COMPARISON

Throughout the ages, we as women have gone from close-knit groups of friends around 50 women (at the most) to around 5000. So chances are, you will have many more comparisons to make. It's easy to look at the people around us, both in real life and on social media, and compare ourselves. In every single way. This is one of the big hurdles holding us back from genuine female friendships. If you see them as an enemy, you'll never really see them as an ally.

There comes a time, where we have to break down the illusion of success. It's so important to refine and define what the word 'success' even means. Success for some is having a baby, success for others is an impressive property portfolio. Damn, success for some is getting out of bed after an episode of depression. Not to say that our favourite speaker or inspiration isn't successful, but remember what you *don't* see.

If you must compare, be real about it. There is an entire journey towards success and one person's definition of success is not the same for someone else.

There are simple steps in identifying what success means to you:

- Do you want to follow their path or yours?
- How have you overcome your hardest hurdles?
- Are you in the pursuit of your own happiness?
- Are you willing to fall in love with yourself?

A book I love to read is *The Dark Nights of the Soul,* written by legend Thomas Moore. In this book, he describes how to navigate life's ordeals, from the loss of a loved one, the end of a relationship, aging and illness, to career disappointments or just feeling a massive shortage in happiness. Success is subjective. Whether you have landed a promotion, hit a one-year anniversary with your partner, or slept eight hours with a newborn, if you feel good about it, feel proud about it.

I have experienced a lot of trauma and loss in my life. However, I do believe each time we break, we expand.

I remember the passing of my beloved grandmother Joan. I was only a girl but my world completely shifted with her departure. Life is made up of a series of moments and, in reality, they all pass. For a young girl without the life experiences I have today, I couldn't understand my grief, and worse still, I couldn't express it.

The 'dark night of the soul' has been spoken about for many, many years. The premise and legacy surrounding the dark night of the soul, is about the synergy between a person's breaking point and subsequent enlightenment (a breakthrough!). I feel I have experienced dark nights like this several times in my life, but it wasn't until I started to read more deeply about it that I began to really understand the experience. These points in our lives are our own 'hero's journey', a term coined by writer Joseph Campbell. For me, the dark night of the soul is essentially a death; between hardship and rebirth. It's a painful and arduous lesson to learn, but it can also be incredibly magical. If you can hang in there and face yourself in the moment, please do it! Like *really* do it. Just imagine how life could look through a different lens? Pretty spectacular I'm sure.

I remember being in Los Angeles and completely running out of money, wondering how I got to this place. I had no work, no finances to live on and I was incredibly lonely. I had fallen into a depression and an existential crisis all at once. Why was I here? What was my life's work? What was my contribution and purpose in this world? One version of the dark night of the soul experience had begun.

My next experience of a dark night of the soul happened months after this when I travelled to Mogadishu, Somalia, while filming the documentary *Go Back to Where you Came From*. After living in LA and then finding myself on a journey in a country considered to be the most dangerous city in the world (at the time), I knew I was facing a challenge.

I was in a city that had been torn apart at the seams. It was lawless, without a government and there were people standing with guns everywhere. With death, destruction and poverty as far as your eyes could see, I was in a world far away from the beaches of California and the riches of the Hollywood Hills. I did not feel safe at all. I questioned, 'How could this be? How could this be fair? And what was my part in any of this?' After a long day of visiting poverty-stricken tent cities and driving through streets with shops and homes that had been completely destroyed, the worst was yet to come. We arrived at a makeshift baby health centre and food bank. The mothers lined up to weigh their tiny babies in a bucket on a rope. All of the babies had heads larger than their tiny stick-thin bodies, swollen hunger-stricken bellies and large sunken eyes. Their broken-hearted mothers held them.

I remember asking a mother the age of her newborn. I was told that she was in fact over twelve months old and probably would not live much longer due to malnourishment and stunted development. This was the true, dark gravity of what was happening in this child's city. She would be one of many children who would lose their lives.

I held on to my tears until we had left the centre. We walked the nearby streets (what was left of them) and as the tears streamed down my face, I was forced to step over a dead dog's body. A stiff, furry and lifeless body with protruding ribs. This is not something I would have seen in Los Angeles or at home in Australia but in Mogadishu, the streets were littered with signs of death.

On this particular night, my world and soul shifted. I physically felt like the world was falling away from me. I was overwhelmed by feelings of grief and anger. I was in a deep and dark pit of despair recollecting the atrocities I witnessed in Somalia. The world seemed utterly unfair, unbalanced and I felt completely helpless.

In that moment, I chose to follow the calling from the darkness to the light, and find a new direction in life. I knew my soul was choosing to step out of the competition and the comparison of the entertainment industry (as I knew it) and follow a different calling. Some might call it an awakening to my soul's true purpose and desire. So, my 'dark night of the soul' illuminated with absolute intention.

Ironically, it was surrendering to my past that made me think about comparison and competition, and the role the two 'C's had on me and my life. I would go as far as to say that competition can often be mistaken for healthy desire. It was in Somalia, I realised that my career to date could be put to good use. After all, desire for anything positive can be rewarding and purposeful.

However, it's important to understand the nature of a competitive culture in our lives; in our homes, our relationships and our professional pursuits.

A competitive culture promotes two things, the winners and the losers. This, for me, has been a hurdle to overcome. When I was a model, there were times where I felt embarrassed or sad when I wasn't the best in the room. Like other aspects of my life, I felt like an athlete. I worked hard to achieve a shape or look, or be skilled. Coming from a career in modelling and acting, it was all about competition. In my determination in landing a modelling campaign, or being cast in a show, my celebrity status allowed me the platform to speak up about human and animal rights. This is where competition can do good. Competition is actually a healthy measuring stick when striving for something bigger, something better. Removing the ego, means competition can unravel positively.

Nowadays, women are becoming increasingly stronger in the workplace. This is also a good thing! Gender pay gaps are improving, and women are becoming the leaders of nations. But this hasn't happened without some serious competition. If you are not an aspiring prime minister or president, competition can still exist closer to home. This could look like setting up a local book club, a charity or small business. Success and competition can exist closely together, and in some ways they need to.

As someone who inspires, trains and mentors Circle Facilitators globally, I urge women to lead from the front, to rally and motivate. But the one key message on how to be kind in a competitive culture, is to understand your intentions, commit to compassionate leadership and never leave anyone behind.

Every morning, I sit in front of a window, with my daughter on my lap. Together, we have this morning ritual that includes our daily affirmations.

We say,

'Good morning sun, good morning sky, good morning plants and trees and animals, good morning people, we love you and we are so grateful for this day.'

Then we ask ourselves:

'Do we like ourselves today?' 'Yes, we do.'

'Do we *love* ourselves today?' 'Yes, we do.'

'Will we love ourselves tomorrow?' 'Yes, we will.'

And after a brief pause, I say:

'I love my brain, I love my heart, I love my soul, I love my body, I love my face, I love my hair, I love my everything! Because I love myself!' (By this point, my daughter is joyfully shouting.)

Keep healing simply. There are enough pressures around us, without having to heal our pasts in one day. Take one moment, one baby step, at a time.

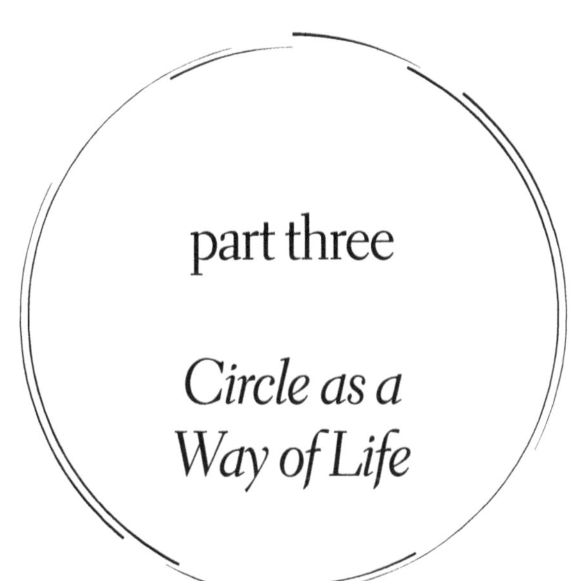

part three

Circle as a Way of Life

chapter thirty-seven

CIRCLE IS ONE HABIT YOU SHOULDN'T QUIT

Circle isn't like a new diet you should try for six weeks and then ditch for the next big thing. It's super easy to get sucked into a trendy new way of living, only to find something 'sparklier' down the track.

When we need something extra in our lives, we order a stack of self-help books from Amazon and buy an unlimited class pass at our local gym to kickstart our plan for a better life. The only problem here is that we want instant results ... and Circle doesn't work that way.

Don't get me wrong, I have been guilty of bailing on a new diet, exercise routine or spiritual immersion because I didn't see the instant results that I wanted. Even when I did see my body slimming down quicker than what is considered 'healthy loss', I would fixate on whatever was working to further reduce my body weight. A toxic goal like this only leads to disappointment, self-esteem crashes and a sense of failure. As if feeling unhappy in our skin isn't bad enough to begin with, we layer on extra guilt when overnight transformation does not occur.

When we get a glimpse of ourselves in the mirror, or see our relationship going downhill, we want to remedy a bad situation, fast. Typically, women give up on a diet around the five-week mark because only one goal is being addressed, to lose weight. And this is a pretty solid goal. But being in an unhappy state goes well beyond a five-day meal plan. Even though the scales say one thing (I threw mine out years ago!), our mental health is saying another. So, we bail and try something else.

For holistic happiness, we need to go so much deeper than calorie counting and 'carb-busting'. We need to throw ourselves into a safe haven; so instead of altering ourselves, we learn to seek acceptance. Instead of pushing upstream, we need to sit in the stream and discover ways and people who champion our current state of living.

Circle is a lifestyle and not an overnight cure. It has no duration of success, or dress code. When you find your soul family, love them and be loved, because your mirror isn't your enemy. This is a place where you control your future and bask in your presence.

If your calling to Circle is to make candles, comfort those in cancer remission, befriend those on the fertility path or simply tell stories, then make this the habit you never give up on.

You can't give up on Circle because it doesn't give up on you.

❍ *Circle is not a fad*

Why is it that we find something that works and then we give it up? Perhaps we get comfy with our progress, or maybe we have stopped questioning the role of certain emotions.

Fads happen overnight, and trends are a slow burner, but both have a shelf-life. One of my biggest goals is to ensure that Circle doesn't become the next best thing for women to jump onto for a hot second. I want the message to spread, but for the right reasons.

Circle has been an ancient ritual, for good reason. It outsmarts social media and was never designed to boost an influencer's profile. As you can see, I am quite passionate about keeping Circle under the 'right spotlight'. Coming from a past where I had to stay on trend, I recognise that it was an addictive habit that did me no favours.

At the peak of my eating disorder, I would practise Bikram yoga once, sometimes twice, a day. That is three hours of yoga at 40 degrees Celsius (105 degrees Fahrenheit) and 40 per cent humidity. The Bikram series is renowned for following a specific set of poses in a rigid order in every class. Even taking a sip of water in the first 15 minutes is forbidden, seen as donning a display of weakness. I was hardened by this obsession. I thought I was being 'super spiritual', whereas, in fact, I was in the grips of an unhealthy fitness fad. Not the practice of Bikram but my obsession with perfection and (at the time) extreme fitness.

As a model, I would constantly seek out trends because I had to, staying current is part of the gig. But Circle isn't that way, because it's not new. People design their Circle and not the other way around. When I step into a space, I have no idea who will be sitting with me in Circle. I don't want predictability but instead, I seek out the unknown.

Circle couldn't be further from my once gruelling lifestyle. Circle is soft, adaptable, and malleable to change. When we come together in Circle, we learn that it is a tool and lifestyle, and not a trendy time-filler.

The difference with Circle and the 'fad fix culture', is that Circle doesn't promise results, timelines and outcomes. Circle goes beyond activewear and Instagram insights. Together, it's about committing to the processing, and avoiding the temptation to move on to the next big thing. That is how Circle has been a game-changer for women across the world.

The greatest things in life happen when
you open a door that shocks you

chapter thirty-eight

BE THE BEST ANCHOR IN THE ROOM, *and here's how*

1. Do something that helps you feel like you are stepping out of your everyday self and putting on your sacred 'doula hat'. I like to wear a piece of my grandmother Joan's jewellery as it's incredibly sentimental to me, and discreet. Often, I like to put up my hair and remove my make-up. Doing these things reminds me to be the anchor in the room. I need to be the stillness and support person that the room can lean on. I am reminded to be more than my 'everyday' self.

2. Sit somewhere quiet and private, remove your shoes if you can and breathe ten deep breaths while feeling your feet on the ground. Straighten your spine. Touch your heart with one hand and your belly with the other. Tell your intuition that you are listening. You are now ready to be the anchor in the room.

3. Write a grounding mantra for yourself. I like to repeat, 'I am here to serve, I am here to listen, I am right where I am meant to be and nowhere else exists right now.' This mantra allows me to feel open, present and in full service to the people who need me.

chapter thirty-nine

HOW I LOST AND DISCOVERED CIRCLE AGAIN

Finding Circle can happen more than once. And when I say finding, I mean recovering your spiritual path that found its way to the backburner. Growth isn't a one-hit wonder. It can be a dangerous mindset to believe that once you have experienced 'enlightenment', it will stick forever. Like anything, happiness and connectivity take work. We can take our growth for granted. Have you ever been in a situation, where none of your usual 'tools' touched the sides at a difficult time in your life? Perhaps you have learnt of your infertility or your partner's infidelity, to find that none of your go-to cures worked. You have scheduled every yoga class on the timetable, coffee dates with your best friend, weekly therapy and *still*, nothing is working to ease the pain.

Sometimes, we need to get back to basics, to the original steps that helped us before. And trust me, they can again.

I used to chant and meditate twice a day, and fit a yoga class in between. I would have a jam-packed social diary with my soul sisters, write endless new programs for my business, hold and attend numerous Circles and wash my hair daily. I felt in control, alive and at my spiritual prime. Self-enquiry was a daily ritual, and I would always make a conscious effort to check in with my emotions. And then I had my beautiful daughter, Odette.

Don't get me wrong, I wouldn't exchange being a mother for anything. By now, you know the anguish and fight I went through to become a mother. And it's hard. In the first couple of years, I rarely meditated for longer than three minutes. Yoga was out the window and showers were a luxury. Without my former rituals to pick me up when exhaustion hit, I feel like I am back to my former self. In those moments of doubt, I had to dig deep. To recall the chants and meditation that saved me, the mantras that softened me and the people who cheered me on from the side-lines, the loudest.

I am saying this because I know, it's very easy to rip chunks out of ourselves when spirituality has gone on extended leave. And I want you to stop. I want you to be kind with yourself, and know that what you found once before, can be found again.

And here is how.

Don't be hard on yourself: It is very easy, too easy sometimes, to tap into shame, guilt, anger and regret. These emotions don't leave us, but lie quietly in the corners until we are having a bad period in our lives. They will come at us, poke us and tell us we are not doing a good job at life. Well, I am here to tell you, mute them. Don't give them the fuel they need to survive. Instead, go back to basics. Strip your schedule and start with simple steps to find you again. Schedule an exercise class, brunch with your bestie, and go back to where it all began – with you.

Just go for it: When you see a sign, jump at it. Whether it's a newly published book, an online course, a Circle, or a dance class – whatever it is. Do it. Don't procrastinate, talk yourself out of it, make excuses or put your blinkers on. Nothing changes if nothing changes. Find your edge, and leap, lovely. Whether you are rediscovering the love for a new career, a partner or your womanhood, it's there for the taking.

Get out of your own way: So, jumping off your edge didn't work. You may have edged nearer, peered over the clifftop and found yourself in the grips of doubt again.

That's OK. There is no time limit on discovery as it will happen when it happens. But if fear is standing between you and happiness, choose happiness. Magic always happens when we are out of our comfort zone.

Be OK with baby steps: When I lived in LA, I would practise Bikram yoga daily. People would say, 'Imogen, your yoga practice is beautiful.' Now, I am a clunky and uncoordinated human figuring out my left leg from my right because I haven't practised for so long. I must be OK with that. I am OK with that, because I am willing to start at the beginning and remember it was a process before. And it will be again.

Uncovering the secrets that healed us in round one, can be quite humbling. You can't pick up perfection, but you can become a student again.

'Through Circle I have found I am not alone.'

– Lacy

chapter forty

IS CIRCLE YOUR CALLING?

Whether you want to sit in Circle, or lead one for a small or large group, it starts with a vision – and some useful questions. I have to trust that you picked up this book for a reason, maybe because you're craving connection and more meaningful experiences. Now, the question is: How can you find a Circle that suits you, or how can you create one that could benefit hundreds of people?

When people walk into my trainings and flood my Circle inbox, I ask these simple but life-changing questions:

- *How would you define your yearning?*
- *How do you want to help people (and yourself) in a healthy way?*
- *What does the roadmap or path to Circle look like for you?*
- *Are you claiming your core purpose?*
- *How can we conquer your calling?*

These questions provide a great starting point for anyone regardless of Circle experience (or lack of experience). They will help you to begin to put together a roadmap and start your own Circle journey when this book ends. Let's take a closer look.

❍ *What are you yearning for?*

If we were living in a tribal society, we would naturally fall into Circle a lot easier. Because of overpopulation, and trying to balance it all, our yearnings are often put on the backburner. If you have a rumble in your belly and a spark in your heart, it's time to reprioritise. In my experience, building a collective is more than a side-hustle or passion project, it's a calling.

As modern-day women, we are constantly questioning our worth and confidence. All too often, I hear women say to me, 'Who am I to lead?' My answer, 'Who are you not to?' I am here to tell you that competition cannot exist in Circle. You have lived your life and battled through your emotional elements. Don't start measuring yourself up against anyone now. Your adversity is someone else's survival kit. The way you have interpreted challenges could be the how-to guide for a person searching for answers. The world is in shortage of love, and if there is ever a time to heal it is now. I believe it's essential to couple a calling with structure. Without it, Circle is not fulfilling its true potential, and that underpins how I train Circle-to-be Facilitators. Before holding a Circle, it's worthwhile to sit in one to absorb the magic that is available, but this is not essential. Experience how being surrounded by women can complement your ideas and crystallise your vision. Whoever your people are, ensure that you have an over-spill of support too.

My Circle 101 must-do is create a program and adaptable plan. Some would say over-planning kills the magic. But if you don't feel safe and responsible, your collective won't feel the freedom to immerse in the space either. We have all felt the unwelcome visitor in our life: Imposter Syndrome. Ironically, creativity can be found with a solid plan.

I wish there was a simple spell to rid self-doubt, but sadly there is no quick cure to discovering self-belief. Something simple I have done is that I have eradicated the word 'push' from my vocabulary. I don't want to push through life, a dream, a family dilemma and certainly not Circle. You are not superhuman and, newsflash people, there is no such thing!

In fact, a small amount of 'healthy' self-doubt is a good thing. It demonstrates that you care. That you are determined to honour your yearning.

'The ability to see order in chaos is called creative.'

– Simon Sinek

❍ *What does the roadmap to Circle look like for you?*

It's not uncommon for students of mine to be lovers of learning. But in Circle, there are no qualifications required.

In ancient times, the village elders did not ask the young, 'So, what upskilling and professional development have you achieved to hold Circle?'

Modern times are no different.

Just be your true and authentic self. One question I ask is: 'What are three unique qualities that make you, you?'

Perhaps you have an infectious sense of humour, a love for creativity or a desire to heal through painting? It's so incredibly empowering to know your gift and to impart this with those drawn to you. Harnessing people's joy, suffering and surrender is a responsibility, so use your gift wisely.

Are you human? Do you follow your heart? Have you led a brave life?

If you can answer yes to the above, then great. You are totally ready.

You don't have to be a whiz at business if you want to turn Circle into an income generator. You just have to be willing to learn ... slowly, baby steps work just fine. So please don't worry if you don't love admin. I know Circle Facilitators who love a spreadsheet and some (like me!) who avoid all admin possible. I, personally, am not a fact- or stat-driven Circle Facilitator. I don't do bullet point presentations or scribble pyramid outcomes on a whiteboard. Administration techniques are not my bag and I hope you trust your mind over a marker-pen.

❍ *Aim for connection not perfection*

This might not be the statement you are ready to hear, but it's a statement worth hearing: Not everyone is going to have a mind-blowing experience in their first Circle (or every Circle thereafter)! I have walked away from some Circles feeling frustrated and down, although luckily it doesn't happen often. I've felt like I didn't say the right thing or do my participants justice. I'm only human after all.

We are absolutely powerless over people, places and things. It is our responsibility to acknowledge and carve out an experience, but how this is received is completely out of our hands. I say this, because I know what it's like to want to offer the same spark that inspires us in the first place. But our only constant in life is change, and that goes for Circle too.

People are walking into Circle with a backstory that is unbeknownst to you. Their day was different, their childhood was different and their spiritual make-up is uniquely theirs. Detach from the outcome and commit to the delivery. It is so important to remove unrealistic expectations, and get out of your own way. Have complete faith that what you have to offer is everything.

Me, the women and the world, need you.

❍ *Circle: the right fit for you*

We all attach labels to ourselves throughout our lives, but Circle is a place where every version of yourself is welcome. And you can safely evolve, grow and change without anybody judging you.

I have grown my business internationally because I believe that anyone, anywhere can live a Circle life. Sharing isn't just for mothers, or women who have lost their way. Circle is for all stages and walks of life. From teenage boys and executive leaders to elderly women, Circle has the pretty cool prerequisite that there is, in fact, no requisite to who Circle can serve.

This is great because if you're hoping to join or start your own Circle there are so many groups of people that you can gather with, whether it's open to all or speaking to a niche. As you begin to think about starting your Circle journey, this is the perfect time to think about the perfect Circle for you (for now anyway!).

'I love the sayings we share: "Together We Care" and "Stronger than a Rose"'

– Circle participant

Peace in poetry

Size of group: *3–20*
Time required: *10 mins to create and 2 mins each to share*
Resources needed*: writing materials*

How the activity works: *This poetry prompt is designed to inspire and ignite inner courage and peace. I invite the Circle participants to imagine this poem was going to be read by a dear friend or family member. It is so important, like with any writing activity, to encourage people in Circle to write freely, without an editor's or grammatical eye. This task isn't about perfection, but purposeful peace. It's about releasing judgements or concepts of what poetry should be, and instead, focus on how it should feel. As an example, the first line of the poem could be, 'I am a woman of deep peace.' Once the poems are finished, I invite the Circle to share.*

❍ A MOMENT FOR WISDOM

You don't have to be 'cured' to start a Circle

When people start my course, or work with me to become Circle Facilitators, they often have the same concern: but I don't have it all together! They think they have to be 'cured' of all their trauma, to never get stressed or worried, to be able to guide other people through Circle. Well, if that was true we'd have zero Circle Facilitators.

My insider life hack to you, is that you are never cured from life. We all bumble our way along, hoping that the next trauma or tragedy will be softer than the last. We will all continue to experience life, but it's how we react to the bumps in the road that makes us a work-in-progress hearty human.

If you choose to venture down the Circle path, then you are a leader. But leadership roles require emotional dips too! You can be in the middle of your own healing journey and simultaneously guide too. There are no rules, other than leave your ego and open wounds at the door.

I have seen people crippled by the fear of public speaking. They would come to me terrified and say, 'I can't speak to any more than two people in a room, how can I speak in front of ten?' This is actually a common hurdle. Firstly, it's likely the people in Circle have enough going on, without criticising your ability to deliver the perfect script. They are there to heal, not to vote on you as a public speaker. In this instance, I have helped people add a little extra programming. If you have to read verbatim from a piece of paper, read verbatim. Over time, the sound of your voice in a space will become slower, surer and absolutely you.

In my first few months in Circle, my social phobia was rife. With no celebrity mask to hide behind, I was completely exposed. My time in Circle was a way for me to associate with positive interactions, in the absenteeism of a PR, glam squad. See, while I was healing others, I was healing too. Remember when I told you that I wasn't a hugger? Circle redeemed my belief that I could be a tactile person. As more and more people leant in for a hug, each time, I would hold them for a little while longer. Healing is a two-way street.

There was a point in my Circle career, that I realised it didn't matter where I was because my awkwardness was melting away. I was fully Imogen, in and out of Circle.

chapter forty-one

PERCEPTION NOT PERFECTION

Most people experience an inner drive to improve performance, whether it's at the gym, in our jobs or even in our relationships. We are all goal motivated and, to a certain extent, it can be a healthy outlook to set some targets. But what we are not so good at, is accepting the outcome when those targets are not met.

Whether you have spent years aiming to drop a dress size, or spent thousands of dollars on therapist bills, sometimes, we don't feel any different. Our goals are not hit, our motivation wavers, and we kick ourselves for not getting over the finishing line.

Circle, and healing, doesn't work like that. We don't strive for perfection but settle in perception. I often ask Circle Facilitator trainees, 'Which part of the garden are you standing in today?' This of course is metaphorical, but a helpful tool to gauge perception. If you are standing on a patch of grass with a great view, then everything is rosy. Another day, you could be standing in a different spot, and see only weeds.

It's all about perception rather than perfection.

If your morning ritual is scrolling through social media feeds, then your perception will only see tangled and wilted weeds. Striving for perfection is exhausting. Although your idea for perfection may seem simple, striving for perfection is also an illusion. You are already more than enough as you are.

❍ *But, what will they think?*

A career in Circle can alter the perception that other people have of you. As you embark on a new life with Circle, people may make assumptions about what your new found 'hobby' means. They may have mixed feelings about your spiritual curiosity. And these opinions may influence or alienate you.

You may no longer get a kick out of the things that you previously did. You may start to view your relationships differently, or your goals may have shifted. All this is good, because you are living with a perception of what your future can look like, and not chasing down perfection.

Overcoming self-doubt versus logic is a tricky concept. You may be radically passionate about Circle and plan to hold events weekly at your local school, retirement village or neighbourhood yoga studio. Or, you may want to do one

Circle a year. It really doesn't matter, because you are not being judged by how much you do. It is what you bring to a Circle that counts.

It is so important to be open to a future that cannot be measured, or even rationalised. Being open to the unknown is one of the greatest attributes of a Circle Facilitator, and I hope that you are willing to take the leap, and respond to your calling, your invitation, to lead a loving and honest life.

'I look forward to the laughter and the tears, I feel safe to be myself.'
– *Circle participant*

chapter forty-two

CREATING A SUPPORTIVE SPACE IS SIMPLE

My pre-Circle to-do list is really quite simple. I don't have a complex set of practices or anything too 'woo-woo' before I head into a room to host any Circle gathering. I always ensure I eat first and drink plenty of water. Food is fuel and holding a space takes energy, both mentally and physically.

Secondly, I meditate to clear the chatter in my head. Sometimes I meditate for 20 minutes before Circle. Some days, I may only take five minutes to sit in absolute stillness, silence and presence. I make it clear to myself that I am now entering a space of healing. I place my to-do lists, day's activities and feelings to one side. I don't reply to outstanding emails, comments on Facebook, or voice notes until the following day. This time is about YOU.

Think of it like this. If a friend is having a meltdown and needs a friendly ear, I ask my husband if he has time to take my daughter for a walk, or into another room at least. I turn my phone onto flight mode, make hot tea and make the room look inviting and safe. I make myself completely available to the person who needs me. Circle is no different. Whether you are nurturing a friend or hosting a Circle, it is your responsibility to make sure that all emotions are valid and welcomed in the space. Tears, anger, frustration and anxiety are all valid emotions. It's very easy to feel the urge to defuse negative emotions because they make us feel uncomfortable. But in actual fact, these emotions are as necessary as happiness, joy and excitement. You cannot have one without the other.

If you have engaged with any form of therapy, self-enquiry or spiritual journey, to cry or see someone else unravel, is not so scary. Tears ultimately have their purpose. Tears can be the river that creativity flows from.

The more you focus on being an anchor in the room, the less you will feel the need to fix the other person. With this mindful method, people heal faster. Remove any roadblocks or hurdles that prevent a person's honesty. But this can be a generational stumbling point. As someone born in the 1970s, our parents were the children to be seen and not heard – so it's natural that we would grow up to behave in the same way. Subsequently, the lesson to stifle any emotions has been passed down, and so on.

That is until now.

❍ *Do you have an emotional fly-screen?*

As a wife, mother and Circle educator, the safety of the people who come to Circle is key. 'Allowing safety' as I call it goes beyond just the physical. Sure, a room needs to be well lit, secure and inviting. But it's so much more than that. I need to create a sense of belonging, trust and comfortability and this comes down to energetic and emotional safety. I need to apply a set of guidelines and boundaries that ensures everyone in Circle is being held by me. A supportive space does not welcome judgement, unsolicited advice or an environment where a person is unable to truly express themselves.

I know what I need in order to be myself. I know what it was like when I was at a breaking point in LA, and Circle welcomed me. There were no double-takes at how sad and dishevelled I looked. People didn't judge my backstory or interview me for Circle initiation. They simply took me by the hand, and told me that I was now in a 'safe and supportive' space. When you have lived a life of resilience and bravery, the persona of 'got it together' can be a reputation that follows us. Before we know it, we carry our vulnerability so close, that we trust no-one with it. And as we know, that never ends well.

So, for me to re-enact the healing that saved me, I need to go back to basics when it comes to creating safe rituals. Like so many things in life, for me it comes down to boundaries. Your role as a guide or leader in Circle is to be responsible. Your absolute role is to understand the purpose of boundaries and how to apply them.

In my past, I have found myself in sticky situations because my boundary setting was pretty near absent.

Understanding our 'emotional fly-screens' (which is how I imagine boundaries), is one of our greatest lessons in life. When you have boundaries, you can meet people's pain in all its rawness, and honour their paths while protecting yourself.

❍ *The art of unsolicited advice*

By now, you will know that I am not a fan of 'fixing' or unsolicited advice giving. Of course, it is a natural reaction to dive into the 'How are we going to solve all your problems in one day?' mode. I believe that it's in the moments where we *don't* offer advice, that a problem can be solved. The answers always sit within us. The remedies to cure and not combat stress are not in the words we necessarily choose, but in the silence we can safely provide. It's not so easy, I agree.

It is highly likely that you have offered or received advice that felt like an extra punch in the gut. I am not saying that advice is bad, but bumper sticker solutions and 'socially acceptable comments' can amplify the problem over resolving one.

Perhaps, in a moment of crisis, you've heard one or more of these responses:

- 'This too shall pass.'
- 'I am so sorry to hear about your miscarriage. It's good that it happened earlier in your pregnancy rather than later.'

- 'I am so sorry to hear about the loss of your parents. But, they lived a great life.'
- 'You are better off without that person. They weren't the right one and your great true love will come along when you least expect it.'

So, how could you respond instead?

As a Circle Facilitator and guide we must practise active listening. Our role is to comprehend and remember what is said, listen then reflect back; and be present.

I think it's important for all of us – in Circle and out – to realise not everything needs to feel like a therapy session. If someone is sharing with us, we don't always need an opinion or to offer a solution.

Circle is a place where we are allowed to let all our emotions hang out and be completely raw and vulnerable. So be ready, for tears, for laughter, for joy, for anger, for frustration, for delight and for magic. Hold space for it all.

De-masking modern-day Circle letters

'I didn't know what Circle was and I honestly thought it was just for hippies and people who liked craft. How wrong I was. My friend Eden invited me to come to a Circle and I only went because I

had nothing to do that night. I had just broken up with my boyfriend at the time and I was heart-broken and lonely. I would have said yes to any invite, just to get out of the house. Well that invite turned out to be the unlocking of so many things for me. I found a group of awesome human beings. I had a lot of fun and discovered that even if I wasn't "good at Circle", I was still able to benefit from the peace and joy it gave me. But, as it turns out, I am "good at Circle". I even danced with my eyes closed! I've never done that before! The thing I loved most was that I could speak freely and no-one threw uninvited advice at me. I was wrong about Circle in the beginning, because it has been an incredibly important part of my life ever since.'

– Janelle

'I'm an empath, and probably considered by many to be a loner. I don't drink alcohol and I don't like parties. I get overstimulated in busy places and find most gatherings too loud. Circle gives me a safe space that allows me to enjoy time with other people, who don't care if I have to leave the room without explaining. They don't care if I don't close my eyes and understand that I don't hold hands. I feel accepted and supported. I thought that Circle might be an exclusive place where I wouldn't be understood. I also thought you had to wear a flower dress but

no-one at my Circle does. I was really glad to find it was so open and accepting. Now I go every week.'

– Ashley

A MOMENT FOR WISDOM

Let's cry it out!

There will be Circles where people will cry – a lot. Often, this breakdown is the path to a breakthrough. I explain to my Circle attendees that tears are welcomed. I explain that we don't need to hold a hand, grab a tissue or apply an emotional tourniquet to stem the flood of emotions.

We simply need, as a collective, to demonstrate that we have the capacity to hold a supportive space. How many times have you said, 'I really need a good cry'? We refer to those moments, as the floodgates, because tears can be the product of an unhappy build-up of negative emotions.

What happens in Circle, needs to be honoured and observed. It is not just my role, but a privilege to guide not just one individual, but the entire group. We do not humiliate, shame or stunt a person's sharing. Because one day, it might be you. We collectively congratulate one another. Even as strangers, we are in this completely together.

Tears are a good thing, believe me! A study conducted in 2014, explored the concept, 'Is crying a self-soothing behaviour?'* Results found that crying may have a direct,

* https://pmc.ncbi.nlm.nih.gov/articles/PMC4035568/

self-soothing effect on people. The study explained how crying activates the parasympathetic nervous system (PNS), which helps people relax. The study further explained that tears lessen distress, regulate emotions and act as a calming technique in moments of sadness. As well as relieving pain, oxytocin and endorphins are released when we cry, and therefore can help improve our moods.

The healthy benefits of crying include:

It soothes the nervous system: When your mind and body are spiralling, letting some air out of the tyres can reduce emotional pressure. Storing up our tears bravely can withhold toxins. When we cry, the body is flushing out the bad stuff. When we release toxins, we are eliminating the stress hormones that can rattle us. Rinse and repeat.

It resets your emotional balance: Emotions are powerful. And not just those linked to negative emotions. When we are happy, excited or scared, a good cry restores emotional balance. Whether you are moved to tears from an emotive movie plot, or seeing your child in a school play for the first time, shedding some tears rebalances the body.

Your pain is communicating: The simplest and biggest reason to cry is because you need help. We are taught to leave our emotions at the door, especially in a work setting. However, when we don't have the words to communicate what is troubling us, welling up says it for us. Crying isn't bad, in fact it is a way of asking for help. And I am all about displaying true emotions, even when our mascara is running down our face.

So next time you feel compelled to swallow your tears, please reconsider. Grab a tissue, find a quiet corner, be alone or with your safe person and cry your little heart out.

○

'Tears are a river that take you somewhere ...
Tears lift your boat off the rocks, off dry ground,
carrying it downriver to someplace better.'

– Dr Clarissa Pinkola Estés

part four

Making Circle YOUR Business

chapter forty-three

CIRCLE FOR STARTUPS

As a businesswoman and entrepreneur, I know what's at stake when it comes to launching a new business. I am not just talking about the practical steps involved, but how to back your brand from conception to the big business reveal. I have met many people who have incredible ideas on how to maximise revenue potential. I am inspired by chatting with people, both in and out of Circle, who have so much to offer but something is getting in the way between a stalling project and guaranteed success.

And I get it. In my days as an actress, I would audition the hell out of every casting director. Hustling is hard and it's not for the faint-hearted. I feel the same about Circle. I have known for a long time that this is where I feel at home, in my calling. But I have also known that there is a difference between a warm and fuzzy feeling and building up the bank balance.

There is also something incredible about seeing the flicker of creativity behind the eyes of entrepreneurs. Observing a dream is a privilege and Circle often unleashes a confidence that enables people to take the big leap in life. Because I have built a business on a topic that, let's face it, is somewhat of a niche, I too have gone through the necessary steps that a startup must take. In my Startup Circle, I create a program designed for those who are sitting at the starting lines of a magical milestone. As they say, if you do what you love, you will never work a day in your life.

Let me ask you:

- *Are you starting a business for the right reasons?*
- *Do you have the knowledge and expertise that is critical to your success?*
- *Can you nail your idea and take the next steps to implementation?*
- *Do you want to embrace uncertainty?*
- *Are you prepared to fail?*

If you answer yes to one, five or none of the above, then friend, you are ready.

○

'Who knew I needed a Girl Gang,
so glad to have found mine.'

– Circle participant

chapter forty-four

VIRTUAL CIRCLE – *a big part of the future!*

As I've explained earlier in this book, Circle is nothing new and has been practised for generations. However, the way we come together in Circle is changing – and it's more accessible than ever before.

Circle is available for those facing hardship or who live in a remote area. When I was bedbound for six months during my pregnancy, the only way I could access Circle was online. Many are in similar situations, where it is impossible to travel to an in-person event. If you are lying in a hospital bed, or recovering at home after a long and serious illness, you can join Circle too.

You knew it was coming, and I wouldn't be a businesswoman and Circle leader if I didn't respond to our digital existence. So, Virtual Circle is also incredibly relevant and, actually, I love holding space when I am working with the elements via a screen.

It's not easy to transmit potency online but there are some handy ways, that if you want to hold an online Circle, you can do it from any corner of the globe.

Amp up your rituals: Like with an in-person Circle, I will always meditate, eat well, hydrate, and select my music playlists. I burn my favourite scents, light up my salt lamps and create a cosy environment. Rituals are as much for you, as they are for the people in the Circle. Create the space that feels right for you, even when it's just you in a room, before dialling in with your clients.

Replicate your set-up: I always send an email to all those joining virtually. I send them my go-to meditations, so they can zone out, before dialling in. Offering my hints and tips on how to prep a space and create a home environment ready for Circle is a simple way for others to re-stage their home office.

Post a care package: On the occasions, where I will not physically be present with my Circle attendees, I send a care package. This might include a box of tea, a USB with a selection of songs, a candle and a journal for jotting down thoughts. I tailor the package for the type of Circle I will be holding. Plus, who doesn't love receiving a special gift.

Check your tech: This may not sound like a ritual as such, but it's worth noting if you are relying on tech to hold your

Circle. It's worth considering what virtual platform you are going to use, and make sure you are familiar with how it all works. Is this platform user-friendly, and are your Circle attendees aware of what tech they might need too? There is nothing more frustrating than planning for peace, then having to reboot your PC at a moment's notice!

Create a temporary no-go zone: It's highly likely that both you and your attendees will be joining Circle from home. That means, distractions are likely. As part of my Virtual Circle preparation plan, I encourage people (and this goes for myself) to suggest a 'do not disturb' rule, until Circle has finished. Of course, in the event of emergencies, this rule does not apply!

Be extra savvy with talking cues: It's easy to spot visual cues at an in-person Circle, such as body language and eye contact, when someone would like to share. So, it makes sense that a Virtual Circle lacks similar prompts. For this reason, I remain conscious of who has spoken, who would like to speak or those who wish to not share at all. I do this by encouraging people to send me private messages, flag a question with a digital wave, pay closer attention to those who have actually raised their hand, and simply, go round the Circle and ask.

Get inventive with connection: In Virtual Circle, it never ends there. As I close Circle, I offer letter prompts. Each person will send the rest of the Circle participants a letter. Sometimes it's one week later, or even a year. Intuitively, this letter is sent at a time that feels right. This connects the group deeply and is a beautiful offering for those who have not met in person.

As a Circle Facilitator, it's important that I put my heart into the experience. On occasion, we may dance together in our bedrooms, but that's not for everyone; that is the beauty of turning your camera off!

> *'Dancing is so not my thing, but thanks for offering me the choice to participate or not, in the end a little bit of boogie was fun, thanks for all your support ... Circle Rocks!'*
>
> – Circle participant

❍ A MOMENT FOR WISDOM

Could Circle be that magic you've been searching for?

Not everyone who reads this book, will have a desire to become a Circle Facilitator. You may be someone in the thick of a break-up, recovering from an eating disorder or working your way through grief. There really are no criteria when it comes to understanding the power of Circle.

I don't need to meet you to know that you are a kind soul who gives a lot. You give a lot to your career, your family and your partner. Most days, I imagine, you long for a simple five minutes of alone time, even if it means hiding in the bathroom (or even your wardrobe!).

I sense you are someone who brings people together, although you may be the quietest one in the group. You serve people and help others in need to fill their tank, even when your tank is running on empty.

You may be 16 years old or a woman who has just celebrated your 70th birthday. That is the magic of Circle – it doesn't discriminate. You may be answering your entrepreneurial calling, to design and create a business that matters. Your soul's purpose wants to heal, but a mainstream career in the wellness industry isn't for you.

You may be a mother, single, married or childfree, but you want to be a mother in a different way. A place that encourages equality and not competition. It's a place where your story matters, but in ways, doesn't matter at all.

You belong in Circle. You can lead a Circle. And, in our final chapters, I'm going to show you the first steps to make it happen.

chapter forty-five

YOU MIGHT NOT FIND YOUR SOUL FAMILY THE FIRST TIME

Now, I know that everyone is at a different stage of their journey. Some of you might not be ready to start your own Circle, and some of you may never want to create a Circle business. There is no right or wrong answer with this picture. You may simply be craving connection. And I want to give you permission and faith, that sometimes finding your soul family takes time. Sometimes, it doesn't happen on the first go. And sometimes, it's about discovering what isn't right for you. It's all a process.

Few of us shout from the rooftops and shopping aisles, 'I'm lonely, lost and need to be heard.' If it were that easy, I am sure life would be smoother sailing. We don't always want to admit to those close by, or even ourselves, that something is missing in our lives and we don't know how to fix it. Trust me, this is a good place to be. Change rarely feels comfortable and doing what is right for you, may not be right for others.

Start with searching: The searching can be the lonely part, but stick to your guns, and keep googling, 'Where is my nearest Women's Circle?' You will be surprised at the web rankings for Circles in your area. Pop into some nearby hangouts, or yoga studios. Often, Circle will be hosted at a nearby venue, and perhaps has been on your doorstep all along. If there isn't one happening at the closest yoga studio or fitness centre to you, then asking for one may just be the spark that starts the fire for a new Circle to be created there. And use social media in positive ways. More and more, people will advertise events on Facebook groups and events, and on Instagram feeds with specific handles and hashtags.

Don't be scared to ask questions: I very much doubt you are alone in your quest for Circle. Many of us feel the urge to find a collective of women who, like us, are searching for deeper connections and friendships. Even float the idea with your friends or join a chat forum online. The chances are, you will cross paths with others who are desperately seeking the same.

It might take a few goes: I don't want you to give up, or mute your yearning for Circle. Finding your soul family is like anything in life, it doesn't always happen on the first go. You may have gone to Circle, and it didn't feel the way you thought it would. Perhaps the energy wasn't right for you, or it wasn't how you imagined. I encourage you to go back, or keep up your search. Sometimes spiritual euphoria happens instantly and, sometimes, it can take weeks or even months to experience. It's a process. Stay true to yourself, and that voice in your head that's saying, 'I will belong here one day.'

❍ *P.S. Yes, you are enough!*

You've read a lot about how important combating the loneliness epidemic is to me. Why? Because it's silently crippling us. Nowadays, relationships are fragile. We move in such a fast-paced and overloaded world, that there is not time to thrive, but just to survive. Our part to play in this, is ensuring that you are the change in someone else's world. That's a big ask, right? Or is it your big calling?

If you are punching the air, shouting 'YES', then I urge you to dig deep. Dig into your wisdom, your gratitude, and your moments of utter success. The moments you felt heard, held and harnessed. Be the person you need, because I assure you, the world needs you right now.

I'm not saying creating a Circle will be easy. Heck, we are all human after all. Your self-doubt and lack of confidence will play a big part in the early days. You might be thinking, 'Who am I to start my own Circle?' You are everything, and more.

If you have lived, you are qualified to create Circle. That's it. Be human, remember, there are no prerequisites for facilitating your own Circle. If you have lived through a break-up, you are ready. If you have lived through a love story, you are ready. If you have raised a family or have lived a childfree life, you are ready. If you live from the heart space, you are ready.

If you have felt moments of isolation or a crowded house, you are ready. If you have experienced the depths of despair, you are ready. If you have been giddy for love, you are ready. There is only one of you. There is only one person in the world who has lived and breathed your journey, YOU. No-one can challenge your story, because only you know how it was written.

If you could say to someone, 'I am not going to tell you to let go, or surrender. There are too many questions for us as it is. But I will help you to connect back into your heart and connect back to love,' then you are abundantly, magically, unequivocally READY.

If you can guide someone and walk side-by-side with them without instruction or direction … You are ready. My only ask is to give back to yourself what you do for others and connect back to love.

Because you are enough.

'I am very grateful for the opportunity to connect with all the strong and empowered women in this group.'

– *Circle participant*

Peaceful flags in unity

Size of group: *3–20*
Time required: *20–45 mins*
Resources needed: *triangles or squares of coloured material for the flags, markers or paint, and string for hanging the flags*

How the activity works: *In the tradition of Women's Circle, peace flags have been donated to local charities, hospitals, nursing homes and yoga studios. Peace flags symbolise unity and community. While peace flags have also been known as 'prayer' flags, they do not have to be seen as religious offerings, but a symbol of intentional messages made from love and … peace. Individually, participants will be asked to decorate their triangular piece of material with art or written words that speak of peace. Once all the flags have been decorated, as a group, the Circle will tie the material together, to make one beautiful peace flag.*

chapter forty-six

BETTER BOUNDARIES

Circle safety all comes down to boundaries. When we create and enforce boundaries, we are creating a set of internal guidelines. With a firmly set boundary, we can see and absorb what is around us, but we certainly don't need to accept anything that threatens our physical or emotional safety.

All of these guidelines will help you to connect safely in Circle but, more than that, they can support you when you're connecting with people in every area of your life.

It's OK if you don't like hugging: My family are big huggers. Me, not so much. But I am working on it. My mum would say, 'Your brother is the hugger in the family.' That comment used to worry me because people might think I'm stand-offish. Nowadays, my daughter is helping me overcome that hurdle; to be safe and warm in close proximity. Somehow, it's completely different with her. I hug and hold her as much as she wants, which is sometimes all day and night. I do not love the people I don't hug any less, I just don't always feel comfortable with unknown, physical boundaries. Both Circle, my husband and my daughter, have helped heal this for me, So, if you're not a hugger, that's OK too.

Be firm as a 'fixer': I have always been seen as the 'fixer'. Even at a young age, I was the advice giver. If you dive into family psychology, it is said that family members are all assigned roles in the domestic system. Mine is to be the fixer, the nurturer, the hero – the person who wants to ensure everyone is happy. But, it can become an exhausting role. Triggers occur more in families than anywhere else. In my early 30s, as I was discovering my spiritual journey, I also worked on my self-esteem hugely, when I needed the fixing. When I discovered my worth, I discovered my boundaries. It's not your job to fix the world.

Don't be a one-sided 'pleasure pleaser': Boundaries tend to be learnt but rarely are they inbuilt from birth. Understanding our limits when it comes to intimacy tends to surface from knowing what *doesn't* work for us. We all have a past and more often than not, a broken boundary can instantly break trust. Sexual and intimacy boundaries don't magically appear overnight. They change, morph, develop and sometimes dismantle over time. Being assertive as a woman is understanding what makes you happy. Don't forgo your own pleasure for someone else's. Be desired, and longed for. Communicate with your partner what works and what doesn't. This applies to all aspects of the relationship, even when to turn off your phone during mealtimes.

Being professional means saying no sometimes: Fresh into the modelling industry, I saw the dark side of a boundary-less industry. Photographers would exploit young women looking for their first big break. Fortunately, I only saw a small, murkier side of the industry, but saying the word 'no', was not for the faint-hearted. Anyone looking to progress in their professional career will often work longer hours with little reward. It's just 'something we all do to get ahead'. We don't need to work for free, hustle for low-budget projects or head into the office on weekends to make a point. You can still be exceptional at what you do without working yourself into the ground. Saying no sometimes, is saying yes to integrity.

If holding hands is not your thing: Self-preservation is incredibly important to me and I am not backwards in coming forwards when it comes to knowing my physical boundaries. In Circle, I sometimes invite people to hold hands, sit side-by-side with a stranger or perhaps even lie down. Lying down with your eyes closed is an intensely intimate practice. As a Circle Facilitator, my instructions are never assumptions. It is my role to provide options. Perhaps holding hands is not your thing and that is totally OK. In this situation, I would invite the person to sit cross-legged, with their palms facing up and open. You don't have to be tactile to be kind and open in situations.

Spiritual boundaries are a thing: When it comes to spiritual boundaries, we often go down the 'woo-woo' path. Within the wellness space, gurus are everywhere. We think to ourselves, 'This person has said that so it must be right.' But what is right for one person, isn't necessarily right for another. We need to understand our spiritual parameters like we would the plot of land around our house. We can float away with the fairies and still keep our wits about us. We can energetically immerse ourselves, but never should we blindly follow. At every Circle, I have a list of handy experts on a sheet of paper in case I need to refer someone in need to them: therapists, child psychologists, massage therapists, reiki healers and good GPs. Every single person deserves the best possible care and that may not always be me.

... just breathe

I personally never overshare in Circle, which doesn't mean I don't share, it just means I don't make it about me. I set intentions, I'm aware of everyone else there, and I trust I'll get what I need from listening to other people too. Most importantly, I breathe. It is possible to control a situation with breath and we can all do it. It becomes an infectious tool when setting boundaries. If you breathe in rhythm, others will breathe with you.

It's a great experiment and I encourage you to try it. If you are on a coffee date with a friend, find a place where the energy is soft and quiet. Don't overload yourself with caffeine so your speech and breathing becomes fast. It's incredible how anxiety spreads like wildfire. Be calm and breathe, and see if the atmosphere between you calms. Together, you may be surprised how much more open and connected you both feel.

De-masking modern-day Circle letters

'My mother used to talk about me joining her at Church Circle, but that was the last place I'd want to go. I am not into knitting or baking, and I don't want to talk about the Bible. But, I knew I wanted to go to "something". Then, I got invited to a Women's Circle at my yoga studio. My first thought was, "Oh no, not one of those Circles again," but my teacher encouraged us to go, to support one of our fellow yogis who was starting Circle up as a small business. I do like to support local

businesses, so I decided to try it once. I was pleasantly surprised; no knitting, no baking and no Bible talk. We did breathwork, yoga and journalling. We spoke about what it means to be a woman of courage and wrote letters to our future selves. I found the evening to be recharging, quite magical and really heart opening. It was nothing like I had pictured. Although I confess, I ate a yummy cookie baked by the facilitator at the end (not very yogi of me perhaps!). I giggled when tea and biscuits were offered but by this point, I was enjoying myself so much. I knew I had nothing to fear. I took my mum to the next one. Then she took a friend from her Church. So now, we all love Circle.'

– Ester

'When my husband of 26 years and I got divorced, my world collapsed. I realised I had put all of myself into my marriage and raising children. I had nothing left for me. I lost friends and family, that came with the marriage, when it disintegrated. I was left completely alone. I saw a sign for a Circle being held at my local community centre. I remember thinking, "I'm too old to go" and in my day Circles were only for spiritual people and the Country Women's Association. That is not me. After weeks of walking by the poster, I decided I would go. I had no friends and because my husband and I had recently moved to a new city before we separated, I hadn't even had a chance to find my feet. When I

was married I had no time to go to things on my own anyway. I know now, I was just scared to try something new. I eventually went along and the Circle was an hour and a half long. We sat in seats in a Circle and there was a candle in the centre. It was nice that I could look at that candle when I started to feel unsure about what would happen next. We spoke, we laughed and we did some art. All of the women were kind and to my surprise, I met another lady my age who had also recently divorced. We are now friends outside of Circle. We meditated and that is a practice I now use daily. I don't think I would have tried meditation without going to Circle. Both Circle and the meditation were easier and better for me than I could have ever imagined. I hope all women get to try it. With love.'

❍ A MOMENT FOR WISDOM

Find your Circle props

Have you ever been in a group discussion where people are talking over one another? Instead of sharing a dilemma in a calming and supportive space, we have people vying for air time. Most of the time, these chaotic convos come from the best of intentions, however, we are left feeling deflated and even more stressed out than we were to start with. We become primed with planning a scripted response and have muted what the other person is saying.

We all do it, and rightly or wrongly, it dents how we interact with the people around us. For instance, when public speaking beckons us. In the days of public speaking, I quietly nodded as I acknowledged the speaker before me. But inside, I was rehearsing my lines and completely disengaged from what I was 'claiming' to hear.

Active listening and intentional sharing isn't that easy. Enter the 'talking stick'. I know, it sounds almost childlike to bring props into a conversation to moderate our inner-oversharer, but sometimes, basic knowledge is best. It's an old Native American custom and concept, that when a person is holding the talking stick, only they have the right to speak.

The benefits, however, go beyond just the speaker and some special moments happen when we prop up Circle:

We learn to listen: When a person holds the talking stick, they are sending us a signal to listen. In turn, we learn to truly listen and be present to their words, and not wait for the next gap to speak.

We learn to wait our turn: Patience is a quality that is very hard to muster. But patience allows time for our thoughts and feelings to land. In this busy world of instant everything, waiting our turn can be a timeless tradition.

A talking stick can slow down conversation: The pace becomes purposeful. When only one person is sharing, we allow ourselves time to think, consider and mould a meaningful response.

We might learn something new: Our competitive culture sadly demands a lot from people. We have become so determined to impress, that we block our receptors to learn. When our time is spent absorbing, we are opening our channels to so much more.

We might find some new respect for people we associate with: It's polite. By giving someone the space to talk and share, we are respecting their bravery and openness. That deserves a very quiet round of applause (only when you have the talking stick).

chapter forty-seven

IT ALL COMES BACK TO LOVE!

Gosh, if I could change our world, I would eradicate hunger, poverty, homelessness, cruelty, and destruction by war. Because I hope that love will always outweigh evil. I would spread my Circle message far and wide. I will ... and so can you!

I can feel my voice cracking as I read this aloud to myself.

It's been a big process putting my heart onto paper to write this book. But it's worth it, if it becomes the springboard you need to bring Circle into your life, and share it with other people.

I hope that, by the time my daughter grows older, Circle will be a normal part of people's lives, just as meditation has become mainstream again – an ancient tradition, which is helping to heal the modern world.

Because essentially, it's all just love.

Sometimes, I think we have become immune to a deeper sense of love. Of course, it's important to demonstrate love to the people who are close to us. We need to usher love from the parts of life that have become stagnant and routine. I know that we are all 'works in progress' and I am not exempt from that. But I wish we were less in our phones, and more in our hearts. The hardest part of any human journey however, is self-love. This is not an indulgence, because believe me, the world could do with some hope and love too.

But, it has to start somewhere. I grew up never truly understanding what it meant to love thy self. I knew that I was meant to, but I didn't know how. If we don't know how to nurture ourselves, what chance does the world have? What chance do poverty-stricken, war-torn countries have, if we don't start leading with love? I am throwing out a lot of questions, because it's that time in the book where I need us to look at Circle as something bigger than an actual circle.

So, from me to you, I invite you to see Circle as love. Big, yummy, boundless love.

I want you to fall in love with more than what you think you need.

I want you to fall in love with yourself.

I want you to love and be loved by your family and friends, for all of their flaws (and yours).

I want you to eat great food and love the body that carries you each day.

I want you to feel and move your body, or how you can't.

I want you to call that friend you've not spoken to for a while.

I want you to text your bestie with a simple, 'I love you.'

I want you to say '"yes' to your next big fear.

I want you to sleep past your alarm at least once this week.

I want you to walk barefoot in grass (or sand).

I want you to write a list of the things you love about yourself (with zero ick factor!).

I want you to connect so deeply and proudly with your heart.

If we connect more to love, we can be present, let go and surrender.

It all starts with love.

Circle after all, is love.

'I want to thank each cherished connection that I have made in our Circle. Ladies you have filled my vessel, brought me joy and helped me to follow my dreams.'

– Circle participant

Storytelling to a peaceful place

Size of group: *3–20*
Time required: *20–60 minutes (depending on size of group)*
Resources needed: *Journalling materials*

How the activity works: *This activity allows Circle participants to dive into their inner treasure chest of sacred memories from a time when they felt utter peace. This activity is perfect for any age group, and Circle type. With clear instructions, I ask those in Circle to spend three minutes writing their 'peaceful' memory, and take pleasure in recanting the memory in its fullest; the sounds, smells, and reasons that this memory has become so sacred. Ultimately, the purpose of this activity is to allow the participants to remember how they discovered this peace, so that one day, they can recreate that moment of complete serenity. You may even ask them to share this memory, to inspire others to possibly recreate it for themselves. Be mindful that there may be a person who says, 'I don't have a peaceful memory to recount,' so if this happens, gently say, 'It's OK,' and ask them to use their imagination to create their ultimate peaceful experience as if it has already happened.*

'Any action is often better than no action, especially if you have been stuck in an unhappy situation for a long time. If it is a mistake, at least you learn something, in which case it's no longer a mistake. If you remain stuck, you learn nothing.'

– Eckhart Tolle

A MOMENT FOR WISDOM

The four pillars of life that I will pass on to my daughter

1. Question everything.
2. Have a mind of your own.
3. Follow your intuition.
4. Create healthy boundaries!

I am a mother with little time, an educator with a hundred balls in the air, an over-deliverer and a wife in love. But, wherever I go, my boundaries will always travel with me.

chapter forty-eight

TAKING THE GIFTS OF CIRCLE INTO EVERYDAY LIFE

I'm not a hard seller, but as a businesswoman, I think it's important to impart the business acumen that I've learnt over the years. You're reading my book, and perhaps you feel inspired to plant a little seed of your own; to grow a business that means something to you and your people. In saying that, you may not want to launch a business, or create anything other than your own sense of inner peace. Whatever your future looks like, it's important to know that you own it!

If Circle is part of it, even better!

So, you don't have to create a Circle as a 'for profit' business, if that's not part of your goal or vision. There are other ways to measure success aside from financial gain. As you know from my journey, there are so many benefits to gain from Circle, but if a business sparks your inner self, then I couldn't be more thrilled for you.

Perhaps, you are an entrepreneur lacking the fundamental skills to launch a new venture. The information that I've provided could complement or improve your skills, across a broad range of industries. After all, information sharing is another beautiful part of Circle, so I pass this knowledge to you sister, knowing only you will know how it fits into your world right now.

❍ *Bring on the magic: selling Circle*

You may have arrived at this point with ridiculous enthusiasm to start your own Circle. I hope for many, this is the case. From my experience, Circle is not a competitive movement. I don't see your Circle as a competitor to mine. There are a lot of people craving healing and connection in the world, so the more people who are willing to facilitate Circle the better!

So, let's talk about the business side of Circle – how do you start your own, how do you attract people to join it and how do you even turn a profit from doing it (yes, it's OK to want to connect people and pay your mortgage!)?

I see a lot of Circle Facilitators who are amazing at connecting people and creating a safe space for them to be vulnerable. But their Circles are not sustainable because they don't think of the business side of things.

And, this can be a massive disadvantage to us. As Circle Facilitators, we need to invest the same amount of time and commitment into our business, as we do our Circle and clients.

I know that discussing systems, budgets and profit and loss sheets can feel like polar opposites to the softening and sanctity of Circle. However, it's important to understand that the business basics and your company, is as necessary as paying your monthly bills. It doesn't make you any less devoted to the essence of Circle.

For example, consider what marketing tools you need to effectively lead Circle, how to process payments, form partnerships, learn about and research new activities and expansion. After all, it's all Yin and Yang, spreadsheets and spirituality. Everything has its place.

Circle is enlightening, but it can be a business. I cannot stress this enough, building a business on the back of a purpose, can be the best use of your free spirit and professional skills to date.

'The road to success is always under construction. Profit and purpose (they do mix!).'

We all need to make money – it's as simple as that. Before launching Honouring Heart, I had been involved in Circle for ten years. Circle was and is, one of the most powerful parts of my being. With a background in marketing management, I had the attributes to convert my passion and turn my purpose into a profit. I knew how to market myself as a brand, and as a Circle educator, the formulas are very much the same. I knew, if I wanted to replace my TV income, and remain employed in a career I cared about, then I was going to have to get super comfy with charging in the heart industry.

In the early days, I did a lot of Circle stuff for free. It's not uncommon for those in the healing space to feel a little icky about charging those who need your help. Unlike a doctor, we cannot guarantee the experience will diagnose or treat effectively, we can only show up, and provide an incredible experience to an unknown outcome.

I would offer Circle for friends, causes and events. But I wasn't making ends meet. I knew very quickly that I needed to stop offering Circle for free. It felt weird at first. But over the following months, my wings grew, and as I continued to treat Circle as a genuine service and business, my commitment levels increased also. Not only did I see a shift in me, but a shift in the women who were coming to Circle. When they parted with money, they were investing in themselves, because they parted with money. Don't we all experience a deeper sense of value when we pay for it?

Some disagreed with me at first. I absorbed some very strong opinions from those who didn't agree with me charging a fee. I found myself justifying my income and was triggered by the thought that I was doing something wrong. But I wasn't. Women who come to Circle, aren't investing in me, they are investing in themselves. They are honouring their value, and the openness to improve a sense of self.

Soon enough, my business was blossoming, and I was incentivised by its growth. My close friends, and community partners asked me to teach them how to hold a Circle. Again, at first, I did this for free. It was an opportunity for me to sample the process as an educator. Like Circle, I started seeing the value in training those who wanted to help others.

I encourage you to see your worth, value and time as a commodity, and there is nothing wrong with wanting to support your life but supporting others.

What worked for me

Customer service is everything: *Your clients are everything. Investing in building your connections is key. By offering exceptional and heartfelt client support, you will make a lasting impact and impression.*

Preparation and programming: *If there is an area where I would suggest ploughing in your time, it's the programming you offer. When you create a program that demonstrates care, attention and thought, your clients will receive a meaningful experience.*

Let go of the numbers: *Don't evaluate your worth by the number of people who turn up for Circle. Remember,* *it's not about you. Sure, you need to make ends meet, but don't use the size of your Circle as a measuring stick. Every business and Circle takes time to build.*

Full-time or side business? *A good formula to work out if you can take the leap between two careers, is to consider what you need to earn to thrive (not just survive) and then work backwards from there. The amount you calculate, will tell you how many Circle events you need to offer over a certain time period. I know some Circle Facilitators who earn their entire income from Circle and others who are looking to supplement part of their income. There is no right or wrong.*

What didn't work so well

Getting over my ego: *When I spent weeks designing a program, planning activities and creating the perfect zen ambiance, no-one turned up. I was gutted. I doubted my path, and me as a person. Creating any business takes time, and momentum. Leave your ego at the Circle door, because like anything new, slow and steady wins the race.*

Don't listen to outside voices: *The Circle career is a niche market. Like other professions, Circle is unique, special, and considered less than conventional. Brilliant. Being original and abundant is what the world needs more of. Try to mute the opinions of others, if they don't* *align with yours. The world needs all types of business owners, including those in the Circle space.*

Be unapologetic about your version of sisterhood: *Never say sorry for not matching the expectations of others. Never apologise when an apology is not required. A sisterhood thrives off all types of women. We all as women, will gravitate towards a calling that is right for us. Circle can be a business, and I am OK with this bold statement, as I hope you are too.*

○

'The support, knowledge and friendships that have been formed from attending the Circles this year has been amazing, thank you.'

– Circle participant

chapter forty-nine

KNOW YOUR CIRCLE CURRENCY

Understanding the basics of any business structure from the get-go, will stand you in good stead. We all have a 'businessperson' in us but sometimes you just need the right tools and opportunities to bring out your 'inner entrepreneur'.

Whether you have run many businesses before or if Circle is your first solo venture, I want to share with you the activities and tools that will help you discover strengths, opportunities and most importantly, your path forward.

The eight forms of currency is a concept that most business developers won't talk about. It was designed by Ethan Roland, an aspiring entrepreneur and author of *Regenerative Enterprise*. This concept expands on the theory that money is the only capital worth trading. You can trade these currencies with your clients, and see them as 'trading capital'. Not everything has a monetary value, and by understanding the different forms of currency, you can build a robust business. A simple formula is tackling the currency concept:

- Social capital + connections = influence and relationships
- Material 'natural' resources capital + material 'natural resources' = tools, buildings and infrastructure
- Financial capital + money = financial instruments and securities
- Living capital + carbon, nitrogen and water = soil, land and the ecosystem
- Intellectual capital + ideas and knowledge = words, images and intellectual property
- Experimental capital + action = embodied experience and wisdom
- Spiritual capital + prayer, intention, faith, karma = spiritual attainment
- Cultural capital + song, story and ritual = community

Identifying the different forms of currency, will allow you and your clients to shift, expand and trade beyond the financial realms. It can take time to wrap your head around the process of the capital concept and the outcomes you desire. But trust me, this formula will bring that extra splash of magic that other businesses cannot.

❍ *The Business Model Canvas*

The Business Model Canvas is a written tool and document with images used to map and understand new or existing business models. It is a strategic management go-to used for developing new business models and documenting existing ones, and is used by businesses around the globe. This tool is so effective in understanding the fundamentals of your new or existing business. If your Women's Circle is a brand-new venture, it will help you understand some of the basics to get you up and running. You can apply this theory to a Women's Circle or even additional programming for an existing business.

It is a great exercise on how to approach your calling with fresh eyes and a new mind. But there are always extra pieces of the puzzle to explore.

Identify your key partners: These are any other businesses or individuals that you will need to make your business more efficient and easier to run. For example, you may consider partnering up with yoga or well-being studios to hire and co-market with. Partnering up with a similar business, will complement you and in turn, you can support one another.

Use the resources around you: Resources are means that your company needs to perform. They can be categorised as physical, intellectual, financial or human resources. Physical resources may include assets such as business equipment or premises that you have your eye on. Intellectual resources include things such as knowledge, brand development, and patents. It can be super helpful to invest in financial systems or platforms that relate to funds, sources of income and overheads, such as possible staffing in the future.

Feel the value of your brand: So important! What is your key offering? What are you doing that sets you apart from everyone else? This could be anything from your unique programming through to price points. Perhaps you are aiming to offer a unique Circle experience, or your audience is niche, and therefore sets you apart from the rest. Discovering your brand takes time, but believe that there is only one of you, and this can be the creative freedom you have been searching for. A brand is more than just a pretty logo and calming colours. A brand is the experience and the emotion that you evoke in your clients. The feelings that your clients have when they discover your business is an invaluable, first impression. It is important that your brand translates to conversion, clearly states your core business offering, and tells the story behind your business.

Get to know your customers: How do your clients expect you to communicate with them? Are they expecting their interactions with you to be in-person, online or a different method? Do you want to communicate to a community or individual? It sounds kind of simple but defining your communication methods will set a boundary when you are up and running. Keep in mind how much time and money is attached to each type of customer relationship, because this will bolster your business in years to come.

Discover your client channels: Each stage of the customer cycle calls for different channels. For example, the first interaction with a new customer might be on Facebook or a website. As the customer becomes part of your programming, the communication channel might change. An example of client channel phases to consider are, awareness of your Circle, purchase, attendance, evaluation, satisfaction and after sales.

'I always did something I was a little ready to do. I think that's how you grow.'

– Marissa Mayer

❍ *Your Circle DNA*

This is a great exercise to create and complete over several weeks as you think and meditate on the messages you want your customers to receive. If you take on this task you will be creating a document about your business and brand. The document should be coupled with imagery that you find on the web or in magazines and books and used as a reference for you to revisit as your business grows to ensure that you are still on brand and on vision.

You can also use it to brief third parties to make sure they know exactly who and what you are as a brand.

The visual document serves as a compass for the brand and the business to ensure all activities both in operation and customer acquisition are on brand and mission. Customer experience is critical and makes the foundation of a sustainable business. It is critical that the owners / operators know the DNA of the brand down to the fibres and, in turn, live and breathe the values, mission and personality of the brand. What is your key purpose?

The questions that need to be answered as a business founder for this document are:

Where are they? Geographic segmentation is the practice of segmenting a business's target audience based on where they are located. Segments can be as broad as a country or a region, or as narrow as one street of homes in a town.

Who are they? The demographic segment is breaking down the characteristics of your audience that include identifiable elements such as: where do people live, their income, marital status and occupation? Identifying these characteristics helps us form more of a targeted response.

A client profile: Socio-cultural or behavioural segmentation is the practice of dividing consumers into groups according to any of the following attributes: usage, loyalties, awareness, occasions, knowledge, liking, and purchase patterns. How do your customers engage with brands? Who do they listen to? What other groups, communities or brands do they follow?

A look into their psyche: Psychographic segmentation divides the market on principles such as lifestyle, values, social class and personality. A good example of this is to identify what encourages your target market to transact. This might be as simple as they need to feel like an individual and valued. This will help focus your messaging when advertising.

A little side note: If computers are not your thing, don't worry you can create this document with a scrapbook, markers, images, scissors and glue. Robb would do this on his computer but I'm more of a roll-up-your sleeves type of person. And don't be afraid to outsource or delegate – if you need a helping hand, that's OK too.

❍ *It all starts with you!*

It is so important to understand the 'founder biography'. Your story as to how you got into the space you are in and the reasons that brought you to facilitate Women's Circle are extremely valuable to your customers and your overall marketing. Everyone's story is unique and involves different discoveries and emotions. You should only disclose what you are comfortable with other people reading but, honesty and transparency are great qualities to promote when telling your story.

Bundling up your brand: How we communicate what we are offering to our customers is extremely important. Because we are all experts in our own domains, we often have the habit of overwhelming new customers with too much detail, too soon. The aim should always be to detail what we are doing in as few sentences as possible at the start. We can then go into further detail as the customer either requests it or continues reading.

It starts with a vision: Mood boards are a fun exercise and a useful tool to really explore your brand. There are millions of great images online available for you to collate and paint a larger picture. It is true that images speak a thousand words. You will need to start a folder on your computer or a physical one, to drag all the images you find into. These images might be related to emotions that you want to convey or perhaps what elements your business / Circle might possess. Images are a great way to create a mood or general presence or can also be used for inspiration for you, the business owner and Circle Facilitator.

Catch your clients: Even though a brand is more than a logo, having an attractive, suitable logo is a powerful tool for when customers come across you. Most of us are aesthetic creatures and the right typeface and logo speaks to our emotive decision making. There are a number of affordable tools online that can help your logo creation or if you have set aside a budget, invest in a local designer who can support your visionary masterpiece.

A Circle strategy: It is a word that is frequently used in business and marketing, but the reality is, most don't understand or implement it. It is great for us to have goals and mission statements attached to our business. It is critical for all of us to know how to create a clear roadmap that puts us on the path to our goals, and ultimately, success.

There are several key aspects that are fundamental to all forms of strategy:

- an understanding of where you are now
- a clear sense of where you want to end up
- an assessment of what stands in between
- a decision about how to approach the challenge
- a specific course of action to undertake.

Set some solid goals: As we know, we must have goals, aspirations, and targets to reach daily, monthly and yearly for our business. Some may have heard the term 'SMART 'goals. The 'SMART' acronym stands for specific, measurable, achievable, relevant and time-bound goals. If we set our goals within these parameters and we have healthy work habits, our business will move forward. Most importantly, remember that everything is liquid and not set in stone. Your ability to change things in real time and act with intelligence and intuition makes you a force of nature. Goals are guiding lights and open to reinvention. Revisiting everything regularly helps you identify the things that are working well and the things that perhaps need some tweaking. Being able to take constructive criticism from your community is the mark of a successful business person. There is no failure or success in business. Our failures are part of the formula for our success because without our trial and error, we can never be the best version of ourselves.

○

'My face aches from laughing, so you know it was a good night at Circle.'

– Circle participant

chapter fifty

CREATING A WAVE

Ultimately, our desire to create a Circle is to welcome new 'members' (or whatever word you prefer to refer to your Circle attendees). Our members are our community and the 'why' behind our purpose for those we want to support – attracting your people and creating a wave of love and support across the world. So, it's important we take the time to reach them.

Discover your members/clients ... before they discover you! That might sound odd, but it works for me. It's important that healing is a proactive action. So, write that newsletter, post that caption, and create that event. Your Circle could be exactly what someone has been searching for all along.

They might not know what is missing in their life and that Circle will carry them to a new chapter in their lives. Imagine writing and sending the email that lands in an inbox to the very person who needs it. You have the power to be a true connector and to use the connection to help people around the world.

❍ *Grabbing attention for all the right reasons*

Time is the one true commodity that has become very scarce. As business owners we try to gain as much attention as we can to convey our advertising message without the audience feeling like we are stealing their time. There are a few ways that we can minimise the chance of our audience feeling taken advantage of while we maximise our impact through focused market messaging. So, refining your market is key.

You may have heard of the terms 'client persona' or 'client avatar' before, but if you haven't, this is an exercise marketers use to clearly identify who they are speaking to. Having a good client avatar will give you the ability to powerfully communicate with your core market and therefore open your Circle to new people.

Here is a simple tool that can help you create your 'client avatar', which can also benefit your decision making when creating your all-important brand.

Name: Give your customer a name (e.g. Sally Stevens)
Marital Status: Married
Children: Yes – 2 (12-year-old boy and 10-year-old girl)
Location: Which town or city?
Occupation: Stay-at-home parent
Annual family income: $80K / year

Goals and values: Sally wants her children to excel and she also wants to spend more time on herself and her husband.

Values: Sally is family orientated and knows the importance of self-care. Sally is honest and hardworking but needs more from her days as she is not in the workforce anymore.

Sources of information: Sally spends a lot of time on social media (Facebook and Instagram). Sally reads several blogs related to parenting and lifestyle. Sally has a group of friends who she regularly spends time with, and they share information.

Challenges and pain points: Sally wants more time and more from her days. She wants something creative and meaningful in her weeks.

What does Sally respond to? What are your easy-to-convey marketing messages to Sally? Does she need a break from life or is she looking for deeper human connection? When you are marketing to your client avatar, you are marketing to your community.

❍ *Every great Circle has a great story*

So, what does storytelling have to do with your business? Everything! If you can't properly convey a story, then your products or service are not going to appeal to your audience.

Stories can be incorporated into all your forms of content: blogs, e-books, and even your 'about us' page on your website or social media profile. The value of storytelling can also be transferred to other areas of Circle, to grow your business. Captivate your audience, by telling your story. In turn, this will simplify and amplify your captivated audience. Once you learn to tell a good story, your audience is always going to be wanting more, which will turn your readers into leads, your leads into clients, and your clients into loyal clients.

A couple of key points worth considering when creating content:

- develop content that has a human element
- be sincere and authentic
- ask yourself if you'd be genuinely interested in reading or viewing your content
- know what connects your clients to you
- stories have heroes and characters with unfulfilled desires
- keep it simple, you should be able to describe a story in one line.

When marketing and storytelling collide, it will:

- clearly establish what your brand is all about – its purpose, core values and mission
- offer your clients more than just a product or service, but rather an experience that transcends

- challenge a mundane perception
- motivate the reader or viewer to step into that experience.

This is done by crafting content in such a way that your audience feels as though they'd risk losing access to this somehow sublime experience of being a part of your brand if they don't buy, follow, or sign up right now.

❍ *Circle marketing 101*

Marketing is going to be a part of everyone's business, but it doesn't have to be a complicated exercise. It's easy to get overwhelmed and hit the burn-out button when your marketing is too scattered. It sounds like a simple thing to advise but many businesses don't fish where the fish are. This can be either physical marketing, such as flyer dropping, or digital marketing via Facebook groups and paid ads. For instance, if you are running a Circle for mothers, it would make sense to market in places where you know that there is a concentrated population of mothers.

Build partner relationships: The space that you are in has unlimited partnership possibilities with your Circle or business. There are studios, practitioners, academics, ambassadors, fellow Circle Facilitators who you can partner with to make sure that you are continually exposed to new people within your demographic.

Get talking about what you are doing: Be proud and loud. Talk to friends, family and people in your community about what you are doing. Make sure you have a call to action though. Once they are hooked on what you are saying, offering, and what it is you want from them, you will streamline your message clearly. Be clear and prepared with relevant details, so when they are ready, you are easily found.

Start to build your audience: Social media has given everyone a voice and a platform today. As you know, I have mixed opinions about social media. But, when you are using social media to spread a worthy message, then use it to your max. When creating your social media captions, and content, consider what would grab your attention? Are you your client avatar?

Feedback loops: Capturing information in business is crucial. It is super important to know what you are doing well, and what you could improve.

The idea behind the feedback loop is simple: to encourage honest client opinions. With valuable feedback you can implement changes to better a Circle experience or continue with what you are doing well. We often tie our ego to our business and see feedback as a personal attack, when we should be celebrating it and rewarding the individual who had the courage to be raw and honest with us. Feedback is vital.

You might set up feedback loops as a simple conversation with a client after Circle or seek feedback anonymously. Nurture the information you have because it can only improve your brand.

Give before you get: For new clients, introduce a special offer or free workshop. The content you distribute might be a good way to let your audience know that you are providing a free, valuable information session with no expectation of remuneration. This sounds counterintuitive but days of the hard sell are gone. It can feel good to give before we get – and trust that person will come back.

So, this is Circle.

This is me and my passion for Circle.

Now, this is about you.

With love and blessings,

Imogen x

Epilogue

In a matter of weeks, my husband, Robb, daughter, Odette, Bruno the dog and myself, are upping sticks to start a new life on the Sunshine Coast, Queensland. While packing I found an old notebook with some old resolutions and dreams written in it. I am not a fan of new resolutions every year but this particular year I must have felt compelled to manifest the hell out of that new year. Jotted down, I wrote how I wanted to write a book, be engaged before my 40th birthday, and become a mother.

They sometimes work exactly as you vision and sometimes they don't. I didn't write a book that year, but I am now. And I did become a mother, but not without experiencing three miscarriages first.

That's the funny thing about plans. They sometimes work, and sometimes they don't. Sometimes we have to wait a little longer for our pain to make sense. Sometimes, all the heartbreaks make sense when you marry the love of your life. My daughter was destined for me, yet, I was to lose pregnancies first.

The guy I was dating in LA in my 30s, said to a close friend of mine, 'I don't think Imogen has what it takes to survive in LA.' And he was correct. I didn't. But I was meant to go to LA, because it was there where I discovered Circle. It was there where I discovered spirituality, and acceptance by other women, just as I was. No-frills, no make-up, no script rehearsed or facade – just me. It was in LA, I knew I was spiralling towards a headspace that I knew was a dangerous place to be.

It was a headspace that had the potential to catapult me towards yet more misgivings, moments of floundering self-worth, and the ultimate act of spiritual endangerment, total abandonment to self. When it feels like you've spent an entire lifetime, finding your place of belonging, the pain of the past becomes of such high value. This pain becomes your receipt and proof of survival. This pain needs protecting. This pain becomes your superpower – no longer will you allow your heart to be treated recklessly by others who don't deserve it.

This is the thing – you can have a great family, great friends and still be painfully lonely; still needing more. And that's OK.

It's OK to be dissatisfied, lost, yearning and lonely. It's OK if you are seeking attention. It's OK if you are not sure what your 'next' is, as long as you are opening for life to happen a different way.

So from me to you, for now, my last letter from Circle.

Dear warrior woman,

You made it.

You are here.

You have met you, the person that can have it all (or least, the parts you so desperately want in your life).

You are at the end of this book, and the beginning of your Circle journey. Whether you are choosing to create a Circle business, or find a different, kinder, and more fulfilling way to live, you are exactly where you are meant to be.

We've never met, and perhaps one day we will, but I know the person you are. Or at least, I hope that in some ways, we are connected, kindred souls.

You are curious, intrigued, and have a yearning to discover something else, something more. You are brave, fierce, and yet so gentle with the way you love and care for others.

You have lived a huge life; some parts good, and some parts not so good. You know what it is to be lonely, and question your decisions and choices. Let me tell you this, every choice you have made this far, has led you to this moment.

A moment of limitlessness, surrender and love.

A moment where you yell, 'I am worth it all!'

Choose you today. Choose family, friends and your village wisely.

The Power of Circle is in you.

And for me, well, I am excited for my big move. I want to scale my business and keep spreading the Circle magic. We remain hopeful for a second baby. I have had one further miscarriage since having Odette and I have surrendered to not knowing when another baby will come. My stakes in motherhood are enough. And while motherhood is uncertain and daunting, I have never felt more alive. More Imogen. I have never felt more abundant, more human than I do as a mother.

We need to let it all be.

You don't need to tell your story. You just need good people around you. For me Circle is part of a very natural way of living.

Go gently. Follow your heart.

Circle saved me in more ways than one.

Much love,
Imogen xoxo

Resources

Imogen Bailey

Honouring Heart Founder, Women's Circle Educator, Birth and End-of-Life Doula

https://www.honouringheart.com

I am a Women's Circle educator and I facilitate my own Women's Circles and workshops. I am a birth and end-of-life doula. I am a meditation teacher and a Reiki practitioner.

I am qualified in marketing management and have been in the entertainment industry for 25 years. I am an actor and a television personality and I have always loved what I do but I had a burning desire to do more.

In 2012, I was involved in a show for SBS Australia called *Go Back to Where You Came From* an International Emmy Award–winning documentary that followed the journeys of refugees who had come to Australia. Part of this journey took me to Africa and Indonesia and I started to see something really important. I started to see the community and the spirit of people who support each other in life's truly important moments such as birth and in end of life and also in all the moments in between.

While on the show, I saw women joyfully coming together to get their water or cook meals. I saw them coming together to make things and also to just be. Men did this too, as did the whole community. As you can imagine I am talking about people who are in pretty dire situations. This includes people who were stuck in camps for years and years. The common thread for me was observing the love, the support, the joy and the laughter that came through in-person connections and finding the laughter even in the worst times.

This experience led me to explore what I could do with my life and my career that would involve this kind of in-person connection, support and love on the deepest possible level. So I embarked on a journey that led me to birth and then end-of-life doula work. I fell in love with this work and ultimately the reason behind it, humans connecting to humans.

Renee Adair

Mentor, Womb to Tomb Doula and Educator

https://www.wombtotomb.org

Renee Adair is the founder and director of the Womb to Tomb Foundation. She first began working with women and babies in 1994 as a massage, aromatherapist and Reiki practitioner and in 1998 after the home births of her two biological children she began studying and working as a doula and childbirth and early parenting educator.

Renee then worked for the Australian Red Cross at a young women's health program/refuge in Sydney's east, setting up both the outreach and childbirth and early parenting education programs for that service.

Working in collaboration, Renee helped produce the first research on doulas in Australia which was published in the *Journal of Perinatal Education* in 2013. She has spoken on a variety of radio programs, at conferences and seminars and is a regular contributor for a range of publications, websites and podcasts.

Renee has worked to change the way we think about doula support launching End-of-Life Doula Training for the College in 2021 with a view for the wider community to see doula support though a broader lens, supporting all major life transitions, not just in the birthing space.

In 2019, Renee proudly partnered with Charles Darwin University to co-facilitate accredited doula training for

Indigenous women in the remote First Nations community of Galiwin'ku. She now sits on the official Galiwin'ku steering committee to restore Birthing in the Country. Renee has sat on the Consumer Advisory Board of the Australian College of Midwives, trained thousands of doulas and supported hundreds of women, their partners and families through pregnancy, birth, early parenting and end of life over the course of her career.

A fierce advocate for human rights, the proud mother of three adult children and three grandkids, Renee blends her life's work with spending downtime with her family, friends and fur babies.

Helen Callanan

Mentor, End-of-Life Doula and Trainer

https://preparingtheway.com.au

Helen is a practising end-of-life doula and the founder, managing director and lead educator of Preparing the Way. Trained in TCM and Reiki and with more than 30 years' experience working with the very ill and dying, Helen has deep insight into health and healing.

The death experiences of her own parents, family, friends and many clients and her passion for education that transforms, led Helen to establishing Preparing the Way and bringing her wealth of knowledge to hundreds of doulas, clients and their families and those close to them.

READER BONUSES

(SCAN QR CODES)

WOMEN'S CIRCLE FACILITATOR PROGRAM

honouringheart.com

Use code: CIRCLEPOWER

To receive 40% off your complete

Circle Facilitator training

POWER OF CONNECTION

honouringheart.com

Use code: POWERGIFT

To receive a free Connection course

We hope you enjoyed this Hay House book. If you'd like to receive our online catalog featuring additional information on Hay House books and products, or if you'd like to find out more about the Hay Foundation, please contact:

HAY HOUSE AUSTRALIA PUBLISHING PTY LTD
18/36 Ralph St., Alexandria NSW 2015
Phone: +61 2 9669 4299
www.hayhouse.com.au

Published in the United States of America by:
HAY HOUSE LLC,
P.O. Box 5100, Carlsbad, CA 92018-5100
(760) 431-7695 or (800) 654-5126
www.hayhouse.com® ▪ www.hayfoundation.org

Published in the United Kingdom by:
HAY HOUSE UK LTD
1st Floor Crawford Corner,
91–93 Baker Street, London W1U 6QQ
www.hayhouse.co.uk

Published in India by:
HAY HOUSE PUBLISHERS (INDIA) PVT LTD
Muskaan Complex, Plot No. 3,
B-2, Vasant Kunj, New Delhi 110 070
Phone: +91 11 41761620
www.hayhouse.co.in

www.ingramcontent.com/pod-product-compliance
Ingram Content Group Australia Pty Ltd
76 Discovery Rd, Dandenong South VIC 3175, AU
AUHW020618040626
428152AU00001B/3

9 798318 602283